The Busy Coder's Guide to Advanced Android Development

by Mark L. Murphy

The Busy Coder's Guide to Advanced Android Development
by Mark L. Murphy

Copyright © 2009 CommonsWare, LLC. All Rights Reserved.
Printed in the United States of America.

CommonsWare books may be purchased in printed (bulk) or digital form for educational or business use. For more information, contact *direct@commonsware.com*.

Printing History:
        Jul 2009: Version 1.0   ISBN: 978-0-9816780-1-6

The CommonsWare name and logo, "Busy Coder's Guide", and related trade dress are trademarks of CommonsWare, LLC.

All other trademarks referenced in this book are trademarks of their respective firms.

The publisher and author(s) assume no responsibility for errors or omissions or for damages resulting from the use of the information contained herein.

Table of Contents

Preface...ix
    Welcome to the Book!...ix
    Prerequisites..ix
    Warescription..x
    Book Bug Bounty..xi
    Source Code License...xii
    Creative Commons and the Four-to-Free (42F) Guarantee................xiii
    Lifecycle of a CommonsWare Book..xiii

WebView, Inside and Out...1
    Friends with Benefits..1
    Turnabout is Fair Play...6
    Gearing Up..9
    Back To The Future..11

Crafting Your Own Views..13
    Getting Meta..13
        The Widget Layout...14
        The Attribute Declarations...15
        The Widget Implementation...15
        Using the Widget..19

Change of State	21
Changing Button Backgrounds	21
Changing CheckBox States	25

More Fun With ListViews 29

Giant Economy-Size Dividers	29
Choosing What Is Selectable	30
Composition for Sections	31
From Head To Toe	38
Control Your Selection	42
Create a Unified Row View	42
Configure the List, Get Control on Selection	43
Change the Row	46

Show Up At Home 49

East is East, and West is West	49
The Big Picture for a Small App Widget	50
Crafting App Widgets	51
The Manifest	52
The Metadata	53
The Layout	54
The BroadcastReceiver	55
The Service	56
The Configuration Activity	58
The Result	61
Another and Another	64
App Widgets: Their Life and Times	65
Controlling Your (App Widget's) Destiny	66
Being a Good Host	66

Creating Drawables...71
Traversing Along a Gradient..71
A Stitch In Time Saves Nine..75
The Name and the Border..76
Padding and the Box...77
Stretch Zones..77
Tooling..79
Using Nine-Patch Images...80

Animating Widgets..85
It's Not Just For Toons Anymore..85
A Quirky Translation..86
Mechanics of Translation..86
Imagining a Sliding Panel...87
The Aftermath..87
Introducing SlidingPanel..88
Using the Animation..90
Fading To Black. Or Some Other Color..90
Alpha Numbers...91
Animations in XML..91
Using XML Animations...92
When It's All Said And Done...92
Hit The Accelerator..93
Animate. Set. Match..94

Playing Media..97
Get Your Media On...97
Making Noise..98
Moving Pictures...103

Using the Camera 109
Sneaking a Peek 109
- The Permission 110
- The SurfaceView 111
- The Camera 111
Image Is Everything 114
- Asking for a Format 115
- Connecting the Camera Button 115
- Taking a Picture 116
- Using AsyncTask 117

Sensors 121
The Sixth Sense. Or Possibly the Seventh 121
Orienting Yourself 122
Steering Your Phone 125
Do "The Shake" 127

Databases and Content Providers 133
Distributed Data 134
- SQLite: On-Device, On-Desktop 135
- Exporting a Database 136
- Loading the Exported Database 138
Examining Your Relationships 140
- Contact Permissions 140
- Pre-Joined Data 141
- The Sample Activity 141
- Accessing People 144
- Accessing Phone Numbers 145
- Accessing Email Addresses 147

    Rummaging Through Your Phone Records..148

    Come Together, Right Now...149

        CursorWrapper...150

        Implementing a JoinCursor..151

        Using a JoinCursor...155

Handling System Events..165

    Get Moving, First Thing..165

        The Permission..166

        The Receiver Element..166

        The Receiver Implementation...167

    I Sense a Connection Between Us..168

    Feeling Drained...171

Using System Services..177

    Get Alarmed..177

        Concept of WakeLocks..178

        Scheduling Alarms...179

        Arranging for Work From Alarms...180

        Staying Awake At Work...183

    Setting Expectations...186

        Basic Settings...187

        Secure Settings..190

    Can You Hear Me Now? OK, How About Now?...191

        Reusing Meter..192

        Attaching Meters to Volume Streams...192

Your Own (Advanced) Services..197

    When IPC Attacks!..197

        Write the AIDL...198

- Implement the Interface..199
- A Consumer Economy..200
  - Bound for Success...200
  - Request for Service...201
  - Prometheus Unbound..201
- Service From Afar..202
  - Service Names..202
  - The Service..203
  - The Client..205
- Servicing the Service...207
  - Callbacks via AIDL..208
  - Revising the Client...209
  - Revising the Service...210

Finding Available Actions via Introspection..215
- Pick 'Em..216
- Would You Like to See the Menu?..220
- Asking Around...222

Testing...225
- You Get What They Give You..225
- Erecting More Scaffolding..226
- Testing Real Stuff...229
  - ActivityInstrumentationTestCase..229
  - AndroidTestCase...231
  - Other Alternatives..233
- Monkeying Around..234

Preface

Welcome to the Book!

If you come to this book after having read its companion volume, *The Busy Coder's Guide to Android Development*[1], thanks for sticking with the series! CommonsWare aims to have the most comprehensive set of Android development resources (outside of the Open Handset Alliance itself), and we appreciate your interest.

If you come to this book having learned about Android from other sources, thanks for joining the CommonsWare community! Android, while aimed at small devices, is a surprisingly vast platform, making it difficult for any given book, training, wiki, or other source to completely cover everything one needs to know. This book will hopefully augment your knowledge of the ins and outs of Android-dom and make it easier for you to create "killer apps" that use the Android platform.

And, most of all, thanks for your interest in this book! I sincerely hope you find it useful and at least occasionally entertaining.

Prerequisites

This book assumes you have experience in Android development, whether from a CommonsWare resource or someplace else. In other words, you should have:

---

[1] http://commonsware.com/Android/

- A working Android development environment, whether it is based on Eclipse, another IDE, or just the command-line tools that accompany the Android SDK
- A strong understanding of how to create activities and the various stock widgets available in Android
- A working knowledge of the `Intent` system, how it serves as a message bus, and how to use it to launch other activities
- Experience in creating, or at least using, content providers and services

If you picked this book up expecting to learn those topics, you really need another source first, since this book focuses on other topics. While we are fans of *The Busy Coder's Guide to Android Development*, there are plenty of other books available covering the Android basics, blog posts, wikis, and, of course, the main Android site[2] itself. A list of currently-available Android books can be found on the Android Programming knol[3].

Some chapters may reference material in previous chapters, though usually with a link back to the preceding section of relevance. Many chapters will reference material in *The Busy Coder's Guide to Android Development*, sometimes via the shorthand *BCG to Android* moniker.

In order to make effective use of this book, you will want to download the source code for it off of the book's page[4] on the CommonsWare site.

Warescription

This book will be published both in print and in digital form. The digital versions of all CommonsWare titles are available via an annual subscription – the Warescription.

The Warescription entitles you, for the duration of your subscription, to digital forms of *all* CommonsWare titles, not just the one you are reading.

---

2 http://code.google.com/android/
3 http://knol.google.com/k/-/android-programming
4 http://commonsware.com/AdvAndroid/

Presently, CommonsWare offers PDF and Kindle; other digital formats will be added based on interest and the openness of the format.

Each subscriber gets personalized editions of all editions of each title: both those mirroring printed editions and in-between updates that are only available in digital form. That way, your digital books are never out of date for long, and you can take advantage of new material as it is made available instead of having to wait for a whole new print edition. For example, when new releases of the Android SDK are made available, this book will be quickly updated to be accurate with changes in the APIs.

From time to time, subscribers will also receive access to subscriber-only online material, including not-yet-published new titles.

Also, if you own a print copy of a CommonsWare book, and it is in good clean condition with no marks or stickers, you can exchange that copy[5] for a free four-month Warescription.

If you are interested in a Warescription, visit the Warescription section of the CommonsWare Web site[6].

Book Bug Bounty

Find a problem in one of our books? Let us know!

Be the first to report a unique concrete problem in the current digital edition, and we'll give you a coupon for a six-month Warescription as a bounty for helping us deliver a better product. You can use that coupon to get a new Warescription, renew an existing Warescription, or give the coupon to a friend, colleague, or some random person you meet on the subway.

By "concrete" problem, we mean things like:

- Typographical errors

---

5 http://commonsware.com/trade-in.html
6 http://commonsware.com/warescription.html

- Sample applications that do not work as advertised, in the environment described in the book
- Factual errors that cannot be open to interpretation

By "unique", we mean ones not yet reported. Each book has an errata page on the CommonsWare Web site; most known problems will be listed there. One coupon is given per email containing valid bug reports.

NOTE: Books with version numbers lower than 0.9 are ineligible for the bounty program, as they are in various stages of completion. We appreciate bug reports, though, if you choose to share them with us.

We appreciate hearing about "softer" issues as well, such as:

- Places where you think we are in error, but where we feel our interpretation is reasonable
- Places where you think we could add sample applications, or expand upon the existing material
- Samples that do not work due to "shifting sands" of the underlying environment (e.g., changed APIs with new releases of an SDK)

However, those "softer" issues do not qualify for the formal bounty program.

Questions about the bug bounty, or problems you wish to report for bounty consideration, should be sent to bounty@commonsware.com[7].

Source Code License

The source code samples shown in this book are available for download from the CommonsWare Web site. All of the Android projects are licensed under the Apache 2.0 License[8], in case you have the desire to reuse any of it.

---

7 mailto:bounty@commonsware.com
8 http://www.apache.org/licenses/LICENSE-2.0.html

Creative Commons and the Four-to-Free (42F) Guarantee

Each CommonsWare book edition will be available for use under the Creative Commons Attribution-Noncommercial-Share Alike 3.0[9] license as of the fourth anniversary of its publication date, or when 4,000 copies of the edition have been sold, whichever comes first. That means that, once four years have elapsed (perhaps sooner!), you can use this prose for non-commercial purposes. That is our Four-to-Free Guarantee to our readers and the broader community. For the purposes of this guarantee, new Warescriptions and renewals will be counted as sales of this edition, starting from the time the edition is published.

This edition of this book will be available under the aforementioned Creative Commons license on June 1, 2013. Of course, watch the CommonsWare Web site, as this edition might be relicensed sooner based on sales.

For more details on the Creative Commons Attribution-Noncommercial-Share Alike 3.0 license, visit the Creative Commons Web site.

Note that future editions of this book will become free on later dates, each four years from the publication of that edition or based on sales of that specific edition. Releasing one edition under the Creative Commons license does not automatically release *all* editions under that license.

Lifecycle of a CommonsWare Book

CommonsWare books generally go through a series of stages.

First are the pre-release editions. These will have version numbers below 0.9 (e.g., 0.2). These editions are incomplete, often times having but a few chapters to go along with outlines and notes. However, we make them available to those on the Warescription so they can get early access to the material.

---

[9] http://creativecommons.org/licenses/by-nc-sa/3.0/

Release candidates are editions with version numbers ending in ".9" (0.9, 1.9, etc.). These editions should be complete. Once again, they are made available to those on the Warescription so they get early access to the material and can file bug reports (and receive bounties in return!).

Major editions are those with version numbers ending in ".0" (1.0, 2.0, etc.). These will be first published digitally for the Warescription members, but will shortly thereafter be available in print from booksellers worldwide.

Versions between a major edition and the next release candidate (e.g., 1.1, 1.2) will contain bug fixes plus new material. Each of these editions should also be complete, in that you will not see any "TBD" (to be done) markers or the like. However, these editions may have bugs, and so bug reports are eligible for the bounty program, as with release candidates and major releases.

A book usually will progress fairly rapidly through the pre-release editions to the first release candidate and Version 1.0 – often times, only a few months. Depending on the book's scope, it may go through another cycle of significant improvement (versions 1.1 through 2.0), though this may take several months to a year or more. Eventually, though, the book will go into more of a "maintenance mode", only getting updates to fix bugs and deal with major ecosystem events – for example, a new release of the Android SDK will necessitate an update to all Android books.

PART I – Advanced Widgets

CHAPTER 1

WebView, Inside and Out

Android uses the WebKit browser engine as the foundation for both its Browser application and the `WebView` embeddable browsing widget. The Browser application, of course, is something Android users can interact with directly; the `WebView` widget is something you can integrate into your own applications for places where an HTML interface might be useful.

In *BCG to Android*, we saw a simple integration of a `WebView` into an Android activity, with the activity dictating what the browsing widget displayed and how it responded to links.

Here, we will expand on this theme, and show how to more tightly integrate the Java environment of an Android application with the Javascript environment of WebKit.

Friends with Benefits

When you integrate a `WebView` into your activity, you can control what Web pages are displayed, whether they are from a local provider or come from over the Internet, what should happen when a link is clicked, and so forth. And between `WebView`, `WebViewClient`, and `WebSettings`, you can control a fair bit about how the embedded browser behaves. Yet, by default, the browser itself is just a browser, capable of showing Web pages and interacting with Web sites, but otherwise gaining nothing from being hosted by an Android application.

Except for one thing: addJavascriptInterface().

The addJavascriptInterface() method on WebView allows you to inject a Java object into the WebView, exposing its methods, so they can be called by Javascript loaded by the Web content in the WebView itself.

Now you have the power to provide access to a wide range of Android features and capabilities to your WebView-hosted content. If you can access it from your activity, and if you can wrap it in something convenient for use by Javascript, your Web pages can access it as well.

For example, Google's Gears[10] project offers a Geolocation API[11], so Web pages loaded in a Gears-enabled browser can find out where the browser is located. This information could be used for everything from fine-tuning a search to emphasize local content to serving up locale-tailored advertising.

We can do much of the same thing with Android and addJavascriptInterface().

In the WebView/GeoWeb1 project, you will find a fairly simple layout (main.xml):

```xml
<?xml version="1.0" encoding="utf-8"?>
<LinearLayout xmlns:android="http://schemas.android.com/apk/res/android"
  android:orientation="vertical"
  android:layout_width="fill_parent"
  android:layout_height="fill_parent"
  >
  <WebView android:id="@+id/webkit"
    android:layout_width="fill_parent"
    android:layout_height="fill_parent"
  />
</LinearLayout>
```

All this does is host a full-screen WebView widget.

Next, take a look at the GeoWebOne activity class:

---

10 http://code.google.com/apis/gears/
11 http://code.google.com/apis/gears/api_geolocation.html

```java
public class GeoWebOne extends Activity {
  private static String PROVIDER=LocationManager.GPS_PROVIDER;
  private WebView browser;
  private LocationManager myLocationManager=null;

  @Override
  public void onCreate(Bundle icicle) {
    super.onCreate(icicle);

    setContentView(R.layout.main);
    browser=(WebView)findViewById(R.id.webkit);

    myLocationManager=(LocationManager)getSystemService(Context.LOCATION_SERVICE);

    browser.getSettings().setJavaScriptEnabled(true);
    browser.addJavascriptInterface(new Locater(), "locater");
    browser.loadUrl("file:///android_asset/geoweb1.html");
  }

  @Override
  public void onResume() {
    super.onResume();
    myLocationManager.requestLocationUpdates(PROVIDER, 10000,
                                             100.0f,
                                             onLocationChange);
  }

  @Override
  public void onPause() {
    super.onPause();
    myLocationManager.removeUpdates(onLocationChange);
  }

  LocationListener onLocationChange=new LocationListener() {
    public void onLocationChanged(Location location) {
      // ignore...for now
    }

    public void onProviderDisabled(String provider) {
      // required for interface, not used
    }

    public void onProviderEnabled(String provider) {
      // required for interface, not used
    }

    public void onStatusChanged(String provider, int status,
                                Bundle extras) {
      // required for interface, not used
    }
  };

  public class Locater {
```

```java
    public double getLatitude() {
      Location loc=myLocationManager.getLastKnownLocation(PROVIDER);

      if (loc==null) {
        return(0);
      }

      return(loc.getLatitude());
    }

    public double getLongitude() {
      Location loc=myLocationManager.getLastKnownLocation(PROVIDER);

      if (loc==null) {
        return(0);
      }

      return(loc.getLongitude());
    }
  }
}
```

This looks a bit like some of the WebView examples in the *BCG to Android*'s chapter on integrating WebKit. However, it adds three key bits of code:

1. It sets up the LocationManager to provide updates when the device position changes, routing those updates to a do-nothing LocationListener callback object

2. It has a Locater inner class that provides a convenient API for accessing the current location, in the form of latitude and longitude values

3. It uses addJavascriptInterface() to expose a Locater instance under the name locater to the Web content loaded in the WebView

The Web page itself is referenced in the source code as file:///android_asset/geoweb1.html, so the GeoWeb1 project has a corresponding assets/ directory containing geoweb1.html:

```html
<html>
<head>
<title>Android GeoWebOne Demo</title>
<script language="javascript">
  function whereami() {
    document.getElementById("lat").innerHTML=locater.getLatitude();
    document.getElementById("lon").innerHTML=locater.getLongitude();
  }
```

```
</script>
</head>
<body>
<p>
You are at: <br/> <span id="lat">(unknown)</span> latitude and <br/>
<span id="lon">(unknown)</span> longitude.
</p>
<p><a onClick="whereami()">Update Location</a></p>
</body>
</html>
```

When you click the "Update Location" link, the page calls a `whereami()` Javascript function, which in turn uses the `locater` object to update the latitude and longitude, initially shown as "(unknown)" on the page.

If you run the application, initially, the page is pretty boring:

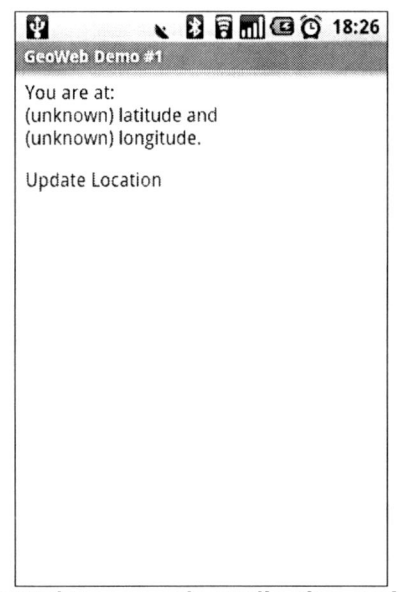

Figure 1. The GeoWebOne sample application, as initially launched

However, if you wait a bit for a GPS fix, and click the "Update Location" link...the page is still pretty boring, but it at least knows where you are:

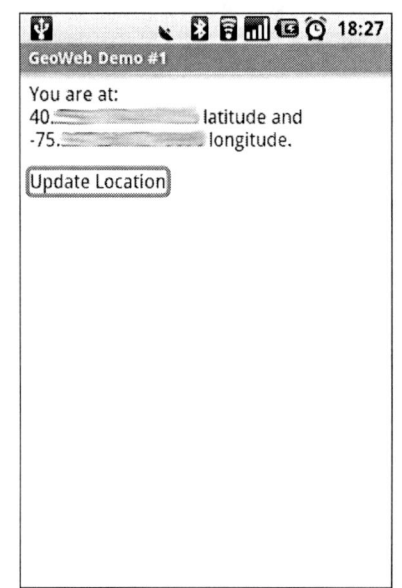

Figure 2. The GeoWebOne sample application, after clicking the Update Location link

Turnabout is Fair Play

Now that we have seen how Javascript can call into Java, it would be nice if Java could somehow call out to Javascript. In our example, it would be helpful if we could expose automatic location updates to the Web page, so it could proactively update the position as the user moves, rather than wait for a click on the "Update Location" link.

Well, as luck would have it, we can do that too. This is a good thing, otherwise, this would be a really weak section of the book.

What is unusual is how you call out to Javascript. One might imagine there would be an `executeJavascript()` counterpart to `addJavascriptInterface()`, where you could supply some Javascript source and have it executed within the context of the currently-loaded Web page.

Oddly enough, that is not how this is accomplished.

Instead, given your snippet of Javascript source to execute, you call `loadUrl()` on your `WebView`, as if you were going to load a Web page, but you put `javascript:` in front of your code and use that as the "address" to load.

If you have ever created a "bookmarklet" for a desktop Web browser, you will recognize this technique as being the Android analogue – the `javascript:` prefix tells the browser to treat the rest of the address as Javascript source, injected into the currently-viewed Web page.

So, armed with this capability, let us modify the previous example to continuously update our position on the Web page.

The layout for this new project (`WebView/GeoWeb2`) is the same as before. The Java source for our activity changes a bit:

```java
public class GeoWebTwo extends Activity {
  private static String PROVIDER="gps";
  private WebView browser;
  private LocationManager myLocationManager=null;

  @Override
  public void onCreate(Bundle icicle) {
    super.onCreate(icicle);
    setContentView(R.layout.main);
    browser=(WebView)findViewById(R.id.webkit);

    myLocationManager=(LocationManager)getSystemService(Context.LOCATION_SERVICE);

    browser.getSettings().setJavaScriptEnabled(true);
    browser.addJavascriptInterface(new Locater(), "locater");
    browser.loadUrl("file:///android_asset/geoweb2.html");
  }

  @Override
  public void onResume() {
    super.onResume();
    myLocationManager.requestLocationUpdates(PROVIDER, 0,
                                              0,
                                              onLocationChange);
  }

  @Override
  public void onPause() {
    super.onPause();
    myLocationManager.removeUpdates(onLocationChange);
  }
```

```java
LocationListener onLocationChange=new LocationListener() {
  public void onLocationChanged(Location location) {
    StringBuilder buf=new StringBuilder("javascript:whereami(");

    buf.append(String.valueOf(location.getLatitude()));
    buf.append(",");
    buf.append(String.valueOf(location.getLongitude()));
    buf.append(")");

    browser.loadUrl(buf.toString());
  }

  public void onProviderDisabled(String provider) {
    // required for interface, not used
  }

  public void onProviderEnabled(String provider) {
    // required for interface, not used
  }

  public void onStatusChanged(String provider, int status,
                              Bundle extras) {
    // required for interface, not used
  }
};
public class Locater {
  public double getLatitude() {
    Location loc=myLocationManager.getLastKnownLocation(PROVIDER);

    if (loc==null) {
      return(0);
    }

    return(loc.getLatitude());
  }

  public double getLongitude() {
    Location loc=myLocationManager.getLastKnownLocation(PROVIDER);

    if (loc==null) {
      return(0);
    }

    return(loc.getLongitude());
  }
}
}
```

Before, the onLocationChanged() method of our LocationListener callback did nothing. Now, it builds up a call to a whereami() Javascript function, providing the latitude and longitude as parameters to that call. So, for example, if our location were 40 degrees latitude and -75 degrees longitude, the call would be `whereami(40,-75)`. Then, it puts `javascript:` in front of it and calls `loadUrl()` on the `WebView`. The result is that a `whereami()` function in the Web page gets called with the new location.

That Web page, of course, also needed a slight revision, to accommodate the option of having the position be passed in:

```html
<html>
<head>
<title>Android GeoWebTwo Demo</title>
<script language="javascript">
  function whereami(lat, lon) {
    document.getElementById("lat").innerHTML=lat;
    document.getElementById("lon").innerHTML=lon;
  }
</script>
</head>
<body>
<p>
You are at: <br/> <span id="lat">(unknown)</span> latitude and <br/>
<span id="lon">(unknown)</span> longitude.
</p>
<p><a onClick="whereami(locater.getLatitude(), locater.getLongitude())">
Update Location</a></p>
</body>
</html>
```

The basics are the same, and we can even keep our "Update Location" link, albeit with a slightly different `onClick` attribute.

If you build, install, and run this revised sample on a GPS-equipped Android device, the page will initially display with "(unknown)" for the current position. After a fix is ready, though, the page will automatically update to reflect your actual position. And, as before, you can always click "Update Location" if you wish.

Gearing Up

In these examples, we demonstrate how `WebView` can interact with Java code, code that provides a service a little like one of those from Gears.

Of course, what would be really slick is if we could use Gears itself.

The good news is that Android is close on that front. Gears is actually baked into Android. However, it is only exposed by the Browser application, not via WebView. So, an end user of an Android device can leverage Gears-enabled Web pages.

For example, you could load the Geolocation sample application[12] in your Android device's Browser application. Initially, you will get the standard "can we please use Gears?" security prompt:

Figure 3. The Gears security prompt

Then, Gears will fire up the GPS interface (if enabled) and will fetch your location:

---

12 http://code.google.com/apis/gears/samples/hello_world_geolocation.html

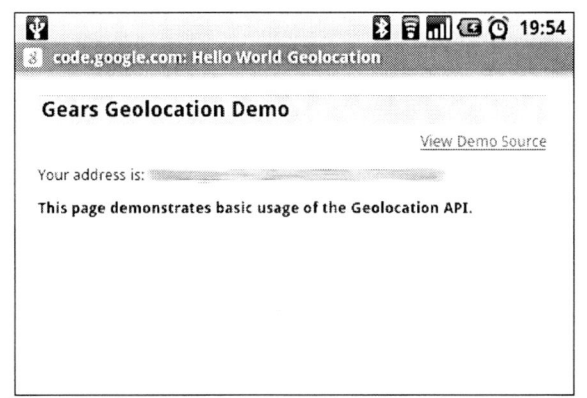

Figure 4. The Gears Geolocation sample application

Back To The Future

The core Android team has indicated that these sorts of capabilities will increase in future editions of the Android operating system. This could include support for more types of plugins, a richer Java-Javascript bridge, and so on.

You can also expect some improvements coming from the overall Android ecosystem. For example, the PhoneGap[13] project is attempting to build a framework that supports creating Android applications solely out of Web content, using WebView as the front-end, supporting a range of Gears-like capabilities and more, such as accelerometer awareness.

---

13 http://phonegap.com/

CHAPTER 2

Crafting Your Own Views

One of the classic forms of code reuse is the GUI widget. Since the advent of Microsoft Windows – and, to some extent, even earlier – developers have been creating their own widgets to extend an existing widget set. These range from 16-bit Windows "custom controls" to 32-bit Windows OCX components to the innumerable widgets available for Java Swing and SWT, and beyond. Android lets you craft your own widgets as well, such as extending an existing widget with a new UI or new behaviors.

Getting Meta

One common way of creating your own widgets is to aggregate other widgets together into a reusable "meta" widget. Rather than worry about all the details of measuring the widget sizes and drawing its contents, you simply worry about creating the public interface for how one interacts with the widget.

In this section, we will look at the Views/Meter sample project. Here, we bundle a ProgressBar and two ImageButton widgets into a reusable Meter widget, allowing one to change a value by clicking "increment" and "decrement" buttons. In most cases, one would probably be better served using the built-in SeekBar widget. However, there are times when we only want people to change the value a certain amount at a time, for which the Meter is ideally suited. In fact, we will reuse the Meter in a later chapter when we show how to manipulate the various volume levels in Android.

The Widget Layout

The first step towards creating a reusable widget is to lay it out. In some cases, you may prefer to create your widget contents purely in Java, particularly if many copies of the widget will be created and you do not want to inflate them every time. However, otherwise, layout XML is simpler in many cases than the in-Java alternative.

Here is one such `Meter` layout (`res/layout/meter.xml` in `Views/Meter`):

```xml
<?xml version="1.0" encoding="utf-8"?>
<LinearLayout xmlns:android="http://schemas.android.com/apk/res/android"
  android:orientation="horizontal"
  android:layout_width="fill_parent"
  android:layout_height="wrap_content"
>
  <ImageButton android:id="@+id/decr"
    android:layout_height="30px"
    android:layout_width="30px"
    android:src="@drawable/decr"
  />
  <ProgressBar android:id="@+id/bar"
    style="?android:attr/progressBarStyleHorizontal"
    android:layout_width="0px"
    android:layout_weight="1"
    android:layout_height="wrap_content"
  />
  <ImageButton android:id="@+id/incr"
    android:layout_height="30px"
    android:layout_width="30px"
    android:src="@drawable/incr"
  />
</LinearLayout>
```

All we do is line them up in a row, giving the `ProgressBar` any excess space (via `android:layout_width = "0px"` and `android:layout_weight = "1"`). We are using a pair of 16x16 pixel images from the Nuvola[14] icon set for the increment and decrement button faces.

---

14 http://www.icon-king.com/projects/nuvola

The Attribute Declarations

Widgets usually have attributes that you can set in the XML file, such as the `android:src` attribute we specified on the `ImageButton` widgets in the layout above. You can create your own custom attributes that can be used in your custom widget, by creating a `res/values/attrs.xml` file to specify them.

For example, here is the attributes file for `Meter`:

```xml
<resources>
  <declare-styleable name="Meter">
    <attr name="max" format="integer" />
    <attr name="incr" format="integer" />
    <attr name="decr" format="integer" />
  </declare-styleable>
</resources>
```

The `declare-styleable` element describes what attributes are available on the widget class specified in the name attribute – in our case, we will call the widget `Meter`. Inside `declare-styleable` you can have one or more `attr` elements, each indicating the name of an attribute (e.g., `incr`) and what data type the attribute has (e.g., `integer`). The data type will help with compile-time validation and in getting any supplied values for this attribute parsed into the appropriate type at runtime.

Here, we indicate there are three attributes: `max` (indicating the highest value the `Meter` will go to), `incr` (indicating how much the value should increase when the increment button is clicked), and `decr` (indicating how much the value should decrease when the decrement button is clicked).

The Widget Implementation

There are many ways to go about actually implementing a widget. This section outlines one option: using a container class (specifically `LinearLayout`) and inflating the contents of your widget layout into the container.

The Constructor

To be usable inside of layout XML, you need to implement a constructor that takes two parameters:

1. A `Context` object, typically representing the `Activity` that is inflating your widget
2. An `AttributeSet`, representing the bundle of attributes included in the element in the layout being inflated that references your widget

In this constructor, after chaining to your superclass, you can do some basic configuration of your widget. Bear in mind, though, that you are not in position to configure the widgets that make up your aggregate widget – you need to wait until `onFinishInflate()` before you can do anything with those.

One thing you definitely want to do in the constructor, though, is use that `AttributeSet` to get the values of whatever attributes you defined in your `attrs.xml` file. For example, here is the constructor for `Meter`:

```java
public Meter(final Context ctxt, AttributeSet attrs) {
  super(ctxt, attrs);

  this.setOrientation(HORIZONTAL);

  TypedArray a=ctxt.obtainStyledAttributes(attrs,
                                           R.styleable.Meter,
                                           0, 0);

  max=a.getInt(R.styleable.Meter_max, 100);
  incrAmount=a.getInt(R.styleable.Meter_incr, 1);
  decrAmount=-1*a.getInt(R.styleable.Meter_decr, 1);

  a.recycle();
}
```

The `obtainStyledAttributes()` on `Context` allows us to convert the `AttributeSet` into useful values:

- It resolves references to other resources, such as strings
- It handles any styles that might be declared via the style attribute in the layout element that references your widget

Crafting Your Own Views

- It finds the resources you declared via attrs.xml and makes them available to you

In the code shown above, we get our `TypedArray` via `obtainStyledAttributes()`, then call `getInt()` three times to get our values out of the `TypedArray`. The `TypedArray` is keyed by `R.styleable` identifiers, so we use the three generated for us by the build tools for `max`, `incr`, and `decr`.

Note that you should call `recycle()` on the `TypedArray` when done – this makes this `TypedArray` available for immediate reuse, rather than forcing it to be garbage-collected.

Finishing Inflation

Your widget will also typically override `onFinishInflate()`. At this point, you can turn around and add your own contents, via Java code or, as shown below, by inflating a layout XML resource into yourself as a container:

```java
@Override
protected void onFinishInflate() {
  super.onFinishInflate();

  ((Activity)getContext()).getLayoutInflater().inflate(R.layout.meter, this);

  bar=(ProgressBar)findViewById(R.id.bar);
  bar.setMax(max);

  ImageButton btn=(ImageButton)findViewById(R.id.incr);

  btn.setOnClickListener(new View.OnClickListener() {
    public void onClick(View v) {
      bar.incrementProgressBy(incrAmount);

      if (onIncr!=null) {
        onIncr.onClick(Meter.this);
      }
    }
  });

  btn=(ImageButton)findViewById(R.id.decr);

  btn.setOnClickListener(new View.OnClickListener() {
    public void onClick(View v) {
      bar.incrementProgressBy(decrAmount);
```

```
      if (onDecr!=null) {
        onDecr.onClick(Meter.this);
      }
    }
  });
}
```

Of course, once you have constructed or inflated your contents, you can configure them, particularly using the attributes you declared in attrs.xml and retrieved in your constructor.

Event Handlers and Other Methods

If you wish to expose events to the outside world – such as `Meter` exposing when the increment or decrement buttons are clicked – you need to do a few things:

- Choose or create an appropriate listener class or classes (e.g., `View.OnClickListener`)
- Hold onto instances of those classes as data members of the widget class
- Offer setters (and, optionally, getters) to define those listener objects
- Call those listeners when appropriate

For example, `Meter` holds onto a pair of `View.OnClickListener` instances:

```
private View.OnClickListener onIncr=null;
private View.OnClickListener onDecr=null;
```

It lets users of `Meter` define those listeners via getters:

```
public void setOnIncrListener(View.OnClickListener onIncr) {
  this.onIncr=onIncr;
}

public void setOnDecrListener(View.OnClickListener onDecr) {
  this.onDecr=onDecr;
}
```

And, as shown in the previous section, it passes along the button clicks to the listeners:

```
ImageButton btn=(ImageButton)findViewById(R.id.incr);

btn.setOnClickListener(new View.OnClickListener() {
  public void onClick(View v) {
    bar.incrementProgressBy(incrAmount);

    if (onIncr!=null) {
      onIncr.onClick(Meter.this);
    }
  }
});

btn=(ImageButton)findViewById(R.id.decr);

btn.setOnClickListener(new View.OnClickListener() {
  public void onClick(View v) {
    bar.incrementProgressBy(decrAmount);

    if (onDecr!=null) {
      onDecr.onClick(Meter.this);
    }
  }
});
```

Note that we change the value passed in the `onClick()` method – our listener receives the `ImageButton`, but we pass the `Meter` widget on the outbound `onClick()` call. This is so we do not leak internal implementation of our widget. The users of `Meter` should neither know nor care that we have `ImageButton` widgets as part of the `Meter` internals.

Your widget may well require other methods as well, for widget-specific configuration or functionality, though `Meter` does not.

Using the Widget

Given all of that, using the `Meter` widget is not significantly different than using any other widget provided in the system...with a few minor exceptions.

Crafting Your Own Views

In the layout, since your custom widget is not in the `android.widget` Java package, you need to fully-qualify the class name for the widget, as seen in the `main.xml` layout for the `Views/Meter` project:

```xml
<?xml version="1.0" encoding="utf-8"?>
<LinearLayout xmlns:android="http://schemas.android.com/apk/res/android"
  xmlns:app="http://schemas.android.com/apk/res/com.commonsware.android.widget"
  android:orientation="horizontal"
  android:layout_width="fill_parent"
  android:layout_height="wrap_content"
  android:paddingTop="5px"
>
  <TextView
    android:layout_width="wrap_content"
    android:layout_height="wrap_content"
    android:text="Meter:"
  />
  <com.commonsware.android.widget.Meter
    android:id="@+id/meter"
    android:layout_width="fill_parent"
    android:layout_height="wrap_content"
    app:max="100"
    app:incr="1"
    app:decr="5"
  />
</LinearLayout>
```

You will also note that we have a new namespace (`xmlns:app = "http://schemas.android.com/apk/res/com.commonsware.android.widget"`), and that our custom attributes from above are in that namespace (e.g., `app:max`). The custom namespace is because our attributes are not official Android ones and so will not be recognized by the build tools in the `android:` namespace, so we have to create our own. The value of the namespace needs to be `http://schemas.android.com/apk/res/` plus the name of the package containing the styleable attributes (`com.commonsware.android.widget`).

With just the stock generated activity, we get the following UI:

Crafting Your Own Views

Figure 5. The MeterDemo application

Note that there is a significant shortcut we are taking here: our Meter implementation and its consumer (MeterDemo) are in the same Java package. We will expose this shortcut in a later chapter when we use the Meter widget in another project.

Change of State

Sometimes, we do not need to change the functionality of an existing widget, but we simply want to change how it looks. Maybe you want an oddly-shaped Button, or a CheckBox that is much larger, or something. In these cases, you may be able to tailor instances of the existing widget as you see fit, rather than have to roll a separate widget yourself.

Changing Button Backgrounds

Suppose you want a Button that looks like the second button shown below:

Figure 6. The FancyButton application, showing a normal oval-shaped button

Moreover, it needs to not just sit there, but also be focusable:

Figure 7. The FancyButton application, showing a focused oval-shaped button

...and it needs to be clickable:

Figure 8. The FancyButton application, showing a pressed oval-shaped button

If you did not want the look of the Button to change, you could get by just with a simple android:background attribute on the Button, providing an oval PNG. However, if you want the Button to change looks based on state, you need to create another flavor of custom Drawable – the selector.

A selector Drawable is an XML file, akin to shapes with gradients. However, rather than specifying a shape, it specifies a set of other Drawable resources and the circumstances under which they should be applied, as described via a series of states for the widget using the Drawable.

For example, from Views/FancyButton, here is res/drawable/fancybutton.xml, implementing a selector Drawable:

```xml
<?xml version="1.0" encoding="utf-8"?>
<selector xmlns:android="http://schemas.android.com/apk/res/android">
  <item
    android:state_focused="true"
    android:state_pressed="false"
    android:drawable="@drawable/btn_oval_selected"
```

```xml
    />
    <item
      android:state_focused="true"
      android:state_pressed="true"
      android:drawable="@drawable/btn_oval_pressed"
    />
    <item
      android:state_focused="false"
      android:state_pressed="true"
      android:drawable="@drawable/btn_oval_pressed"
    />
    <item
      android:drawable="@drawable/btn_oval_normal"
    />
</selector>
```

There are four states being described in this selector:

1. Where the button is focused (`android:state_focused` = `"true"`) but not pressed (`android:state_pressed` = `"false"`)
2. Where the button is both focused and pressed
3. Where the button is not focused but is pressed
4. The default, where the button is neither focused nor pressed

In these four states, we specify three `Drawable` resources, for normal, focused, and pressed (the latter being used regardless of focus).

If we specify this selector `Drawable` resource as the `android:background` of a `Button`, Android will use the appropriate PNG based on the status of the `Button` itself:

```xml
<?xml version="1.0" encoding="utf-8"?>
<LinearLayout xmlns:android="http://schemas.android.com/apk/res/android"
  android:orientation="horizontal"
  android:layout_width="fill_parent"
  android:layout_height="wrap_content"
>
  <Button
    android:layout_width="wrap_content"
    android:layout_height="wrap_content"
    android:text="Click me!"
  />
  <Button
    android:layout_width="wrap_content"
    android:layout_height="wrap_content"
```

```
        android:text="Click me!"
        android:background="@drawable/fancybutton"
    />
</LinearLayout>
```

Changing CheckBox States

The same basic concept can be used to change the images used by a CheckBox.

In this case, the fact that Android is open source helps, as we can extract files and resources from Android and adjust them to create our own editions, without worrying about license hassles.

For example, here is a selector Drawable for a fancy CheckBox, showing a dizzying array of possible states:

```
<?xml version="1.0" encoding="utf-8"?>
<selector xmlns:android="http://schemas.android.com/apk/res/android">

    <!-- Enabled states -->

    <item android:state_checked="true" android:state_window_focused="false"
          android:state_enabled="true"
          android:drawable="@drawable/btn_check_on" />
    <item android:state_checked="false" android:state_window_focused="false"
          android:state_enabled="true"
          android:drawable="@drawable/btn_check_off" />

    <item android:state_checked="true" android:state_pressed="true"
          android:state_enabled="true"
          android:drawable="@drawable/btn_check_on_pressed" />
    <item android:state_checked="false" android:state_pressed="true"
          android:state_enabled="true"
          android:drawable="@drawable/btn_check_off_pressed" />

    <item android:state_checked="true" android:state_focused="true"
          android:state_enabled="true"
          android:drawable="@drawable/btn_check_on_selected" />
    <item android:state_checked="false" android:state_focused="true"
          android:state_enabled="true"
          android:drawable="@drawable/btn_check_off_selected" />

    <item android:state_checked="false"
          android:state_enabled="true"
          android:drawable="@drawable/btn_check_off" />
    <item android:state_checked="true"
```

Crafting Your Own Views

```
        android:state_enabled="true"
        android:drawable="@drawable/btn_check_on" />


    <!-- Disabled states -->

    <item android:state_checked="true" android:state_window_focused="false"
        android:drawable="@drawable/btn_check_on_disable" />
    <item android:state_checked="false" android:state_window_focused="false"
        android:drawable="@drawable/btn_check_off_disable" />

    <item android:state_checked="true" android:state_focused="true"
        android:drawable="@drawable/btn_check_on_disable_focused" />
    <item android:state_checked="false" android:state_focused="true"
        android:drawable="@drawable/btn_check_off_disable_focused" />

    <item android:state_checked="false"
android:drawable="@drawable/btn_check_off_disable" />
    <item android:state_checked="true"
android:drawable="@drawable/btn_check_on_disable" />

</selector>
```

Each of the referenced PNG images can be extracted from the android.jar file in your Android SDK, or obtained from various online resources. In the case of Views/FancyCheck, we zoomed each of the images to 200% of original size, to make a set of large (albeit fuzzy) checkbox images.

Figure 9. An example of a zoomed CheckBox image

In our layout, we can specify that we want to use our res/drawable/fancycheck.xml selector Drawable as our background:

```
<?xml version="1.0" encoding="utf-8"?>
<LinearLayout xmlns:android="http://schemas.android.com/apk/res/android"
  android:orientation="vertical"
  android:layout_width="fill_parent"
  android:layout_height="wrap_content"
>
  <CheckBox
```

```xml
    android:layout_width="wrap_content"
    android:layout_height="wrap_content"
    android:text="I'm normal!"
  />
  <CheckBox
    android:layout_width="wrap_content"
    android:layout_height="wrap_content"
    android:text="          "
    android:button="@drawable/fancycheck"
    android:background="@drawable/btn_check_label_background"
  />
</LinearLayout>
```

This gives us a look like this:

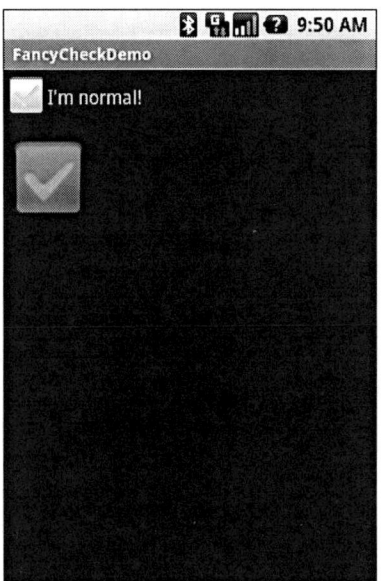

Figure 10. The FancyCheck application, showing a focused and checked CheckBox

Note that our `CheckBox` text is blank. The reason is that `CheckBox` is expecting the graphics to be 38px wide. Since ours are substantially larger, the `CheckBox` images overlap the text. Fixing this would require substantial work. It is simplest to fill the `CheckBox` text with some whitespace, then use a separate `TextView` for our `CheckBox` caption.

CHAPTER 3

More Fun With ListViews

One of the most important widgets in your toolbelt is the ListView. Some activities are purely a ListView, to allow the user to sift through a few choices...or perhaps a few thousand. We already saw in *The Busy Coder's Guide to Android Development* how to create "fancy ListViews", where you have complete control over the list rows themselves. In this chapter, we will cover some additional techniques you can use to make your ListView widgets be pleasant for your users to work with.

Giant Economy-Size Dividers

You may have noticed that the preference UI has what behaves a lot like a ListView, but with a curious characteristic: not everything is selectable:

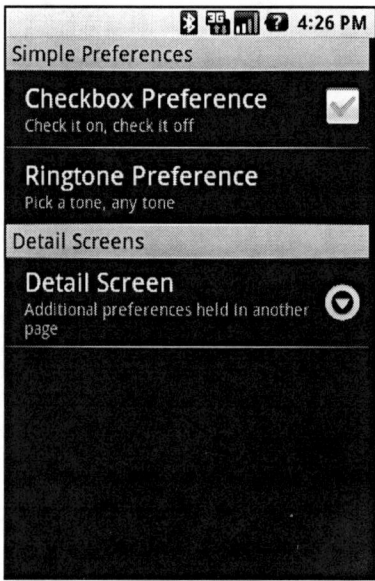

Figure 11. A PreferenceScreen UI

You may have thought that this required some custom widget, or some fancy on-the-fly View handling, to achieve this effect.

If so, you would have been wrong.

It turns out that any ListView can exhibit this behavior. In this section, we will see how this is achieved and a reusable framework for creating such a ListView.

Choosing What Is Selectable

There are two methods in the Adapter hierarchy that let you control what is and is not selectable in a ListView:

- areAllItemsSelectable() should return true for ordinary ListView widgets and false for ListView widgets where some items in the Adapter are selectable and others are not
- isEnabled(), given a position, should return true if the item at that position should be selectable and false otherwise

Given these two, it is "merely" a matter of overriding your chosen `Adapter` class and implementing these two methods as appropriate to get the visual effect you desire.

As one might expect, this is not quite as easy as it may sound.

For example, suppose you have a database of books, and you want to present a list of book titles for the user to choose from. Furthermore, suppose you have arranged for the books to be in alphabetical order within each major book style (Fiction, Non-Fiction, etc.), courtesy of a well-crafted `ORDER BY` clause on your query. And suppose you want to have headings, like on the preferences screen, for those book styles.

If you simply take the `Cursor` from that query and hand it to a `SimpleCursorAdapter`, the two methods cited above will be implemented as the default, saying every row is selectable. And, since every row is a book, that is what you want...for the books.

To get the headings in place, your `Adapter` needs to mix the headings in with the books (so they all appear in the proper sequence), return a custom `View` for each (so headings look different than the books), and implement the two methods that control whether the headings or books are selectable. There is no easy way to do this from a simple query.

Instead, you need to be a bit more creative, and wrap your `SimpleCursorAdapter` in something that can intelligently inject the section headings.

Composition for Sections

Jeff Sharkey[15], author of CompareEverywhere[16] and all-around Android guru, demonstrated[17] a way of using composition to create a `ListView` with section headings. The code presented here is based on his implementation, with a

---

15 http://www.jsharkey.org/blog/
16 http://compare-everywhere.com/
17 http://www.jsharkey.org/blog/2008/08/18/separating-lists-with-headers-in-android-09/

few alterations. As his original code was released under the GPLv3, bear in mind that the code presented here is also released under the GPLv3, as opposed to the Apache License 2.0 that most of the book's code uses as a license.

The pattern is fairly simple:

- Create one `Adapter` for each section. For example, in the book scenario described above, you might have one `SimpleCursorAdapter` for each book style (one for Fiction, one for Non-Fiction, etc.).
- Put each of those `Adapter` objects into a container `Adapter`, associating each with a heading name.
- Implement, on your container `Adapter` subclass, a method to return the `View` for a heading, much like you might implement `getView()` to return a `View` for a row
- Put the container `Adapter` in the `ListView`, and everything flows from there

You will see this implemented in the `ListView/Sections` sample project, which is another riff on the "list of *lorem ipsum* words" sample you see scattered throughout the *Busy Coder* books.

The layout for the screen is just a `ListView`, because the activity – `SectionedDemo` – is just a `ListActivity`:

```
<?xml version="1.0" encoding="utf-8"?>
<ListView
  xmlns:android="http://schemas.android.com/apk/res/android"
  android:id="@android:id/list"
  android:layout_width="fill_parent"
  android:layout_height="fill_parent"
  android:drawSelectorOnTop="true"
/>
```

Most of the smarts can be found in `SectionedAdapter`. This class extends `Adapter` and delegates all of the `Adapter` methods to a list of child `Adapter` objects:

```java
package com.commonsware.android.listview;

import android.view.View;
import android.view.ViewGroup;
import android.widget.Adapter;
import android.widget.BaseAdapter;
import java.util.ArrayList;
import java.util.List;

abstract public class SectionedAdapter extends BaseAdapter {
  abstract protected View getHeaderView(String caption,
                                        int index,
                                        View convertView,
                                        ViewGroup parent);

  private List<Section> sections=new ArrayList<Section>();
  private static int TYPE_SECTION_HEADER=0;

  public SectionedAdapter() {
    super();
  }

  public void addSection(String caption, Adapter adapter) {
    sections.add(new Section(caption, adapter));
  }

  public Object getItem(int position) {
    for (Section section : this.sections) {
      if (position==0) {
        return(section);
      }

      int size=section.adapter.getCount()+1;

      if (position<size) {
        return(section.adapter.getItem(position-1));
      }

      position-=size;
    }

    return(null);
  }

  public int getCount() {
    int total=0;

    for (Section section : this.sections) {
      total+=section.adapter.getCount()+1; // add one for header
    }

    return(total);
  }
```

```java
public int getViewTypeCount() {
  int total=1;  // one for the header, plus those from sections

  for (Section section : this.sections) {
    total+=section.adapter.getViewTypeCount();
  }

  return(total);
}

public int getItemViewType(int position) {
  int typeOffset=TYPE_SECTION_HEADER+1;  // start counting from here

  for (Section section : this.sections) {
    if (position==0) {
      return(TYPE_SECTION_HEADER);
    }

    int size=section.adapter.getCount()+1;

    if (position<size) {
      return(typeOffset+section.adapter.getItemViewType(position-1));
    }

    position-=size;
    typeOffset+=section.adapter.getViewTypeCount();
  }

  return(-1);
}

public boolean areAllItemsSelectable() {
  return(false);
}

public boolean isEnabled(int position) {
  return(getItemViewType(position)!=TYPE_SECTION_HEADER);
}

@Override
public View getView(int position, View convertView,
                    ViewGroup parent) {
  int sectionIndex=0;

  for (Section section : this.sections) {
    if (position==0) {
      return(getHeaderView(section.caption, sectionIndex,
                           convertView, parent));
    }

    int size=section.adapter.getCount()+1;

    if (position<size) {
      return(section.adapter.getView(position-1,
```

More Fun With ListViews

```
                                          convertView,
                                          parent));
      }

      position-=size;
      sectionIndex++;
    }

    return(null);
  }

  @Override
  public long getItemId(int position) {
    return(position);
  }

  class Section {
    String caption;
    Adapter adapter;

    Section(String caption, Adapter adapter) {
      this.caption=caption;
      this.adapter=adapter;
    }
  }
}
```

SectionedAdapter holds a List of Section objects, where a Section is simply a name and an Adapter holding the contents of that section of the list. You can give SectionAdapter the details of a Section via addSection() – the sections will appear in the order in which they were added.

SectionedAdapter synthesizes the overall list of objects from each of the adapters, plus the section headings. So, for example, the implementation of getView() walks each section and returns either a View for the section header (if the requested item is the first one for that section) or the View from the section's adapter (if the requested item is any other one in this section). The same holds true for getCount() and getItem().

One thing that SectionedAdapter needs to do, though, is ensure that the pool of section header View objects is recycled separately from each section's own pool of View objects. To do this, SectionedAdapter takes advantage of getViewTypeCount(), by returning the total number of distinct types of View objects from all section Adapters plus one for its own header View pool. Similarly, getItemViewType() considers the 0th View type to be the header `View` pool, with the pools for each `Adapter` in sequence starting from 1. This pattern requires that each section `Adapter` have its `View` type numbers starting from 0 and incrementing by 1, but most `Adapter` classes only use one `View` type and do not even implement their own `getViewTypeCount()` or `getItemViewType()`, so this will work most of the time.

To use a `SectionedAdapter`, `SectionedDemo` simply creates one, adds in three sections (with three sets of the *lorem ipsum* words), and attaches the `SectionedAdapter` to the `ListView` for the `ListActivity`:

```java
package com.commonsware.android.listview;

import android.app.ListActivity;
import android.content.Context;
import android.os.Bundle;
import android.view.View;
import android.view.ViewGroup;
import android.widget.AdapterView;
import android.widget.ArrayAdapter;
import android.widget.ListView;
import android.widget.TextView;
import java.util.Arrays;
import java.util.Collections;
import java.util.List;

public class SectionedDemo extends ListActivity {
  private static String[] items={"lorem", "ipsum", "dolor",
                                  "sit", "amet", "consectetuer",
                                  "adipiscing", "elit", "morbi",
                                  "vel", "ligula", "vitae",
                                  "arcu", "aliquet", "mollis",
                                  "etiam", "vel", "erat",
                                  "placerat", "ante",
                                  "porttitor", "sodales",
                                  "pellentesque", "augue",
                                  "purus"};

  @Override
  public void onCreate(Bundle icicle) {
    super.onCreate(icicle);
    setContentView(R.layout.main);

    adapter.addSection("Original",
                new ArrayAdapter<String>(this,
                  android.R.layout.simple_list_item_1,
                  items));

    List<String> list=Arrays.asList(items);

    Collections.shuffle(list);
```

More Fun With ListViews

```
    adapter.addSection("Shuffled",
                  new ArrayAdapter<String>(this,
                    android.R.layout.simple_list_item_1,
                    list));

    list=Arrays.asList(items);

    Collections.shuffle(list);

    adapter.addSection("Re-shuffled",
                  new ArrayAdapter<String>(this,
                    android.R.layout.simple_list_item_1,
                    list));

    setListAdapter(adapter);
  }
  SectionedAdapter adapter=new SectionedAdapter() {
    protected View getHeaderView(String caption, int index,
                                 View convertView,
                                 ViewGroup parent) {
      TextView result=(TextView)convertView;

      if (convertView==null) {
        result=(TextView)getLayoutInflater()
                              .inflate(R.layout.header,
                                       null);
      }

      result.setText(caption);

      return(result);
    }
  };
}
```

The result is much as you might expect:

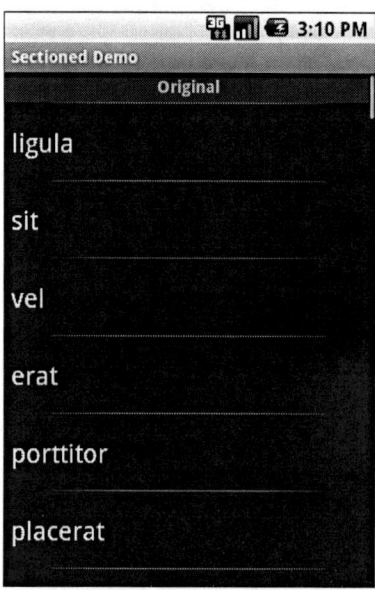

Figure 12. A ListView using a SectionedAdapter, showing one header and part of a list

Here, the headers are simple bits of text with an appropriate style applied. Your section headers, of course, can be as complex as you like.

From Head To Toe

Perhaps you do not need section headers scattered throughout your list. If you only need extra "fake rows" at the beginning or end of your list, you can use header and footer views.

ListView supports addHeaderView() and addFooterView() methods that allow you to add View objects to the beginning and end of the list, respectively. These View objects otherwise behave like regular rows, in that they are part of the scrolled area and will scroll off the screen if the list is long enough. If you want fixed headers or footers, rather than put them in the ListView itself, put them outside the ListView, perhaps using a LinearLayout.

To demonstrate header and footer views, take a peek at ListView/HeaderFooter, particularly the HeaderFooterDemo class:

```
package com.commonsware.android.listview;

import android.app.ListActivity;
import android.content.Context;
import android.os.Bundle;
import android.os.Handler;
import android.os.SystemClock;
import android.view.View;
import android.view.ViewGroup;
import android.widget.AdapterView;
import android.widget.ArrayAdapter;
import android.widget.Button;
import android.widget.ListView;
import android.widget.TextView;
import java.util.Arrays;
import java.util.Collections;
import java.util.List;
import java.util.concurrent.atomic.AtomicBoolean;

public class HeaderFooterDemo extends ListActivity {
  private static String[] items={"lorem", "ipsum", "dolor",
                                 "sit", "amet", "consectetuer",
                                 "adipiscing", "elit", "morbi",
                                 "vel", "ligula", "vitae",
                                 "arcu", "aliquet", "mollis",
                                 "etiam", "vel", "erat",
                                 "placerat", "ante",
                                 "porttitor", "sodales",
                                 "pellentesque", "augue",
                                 "purus"};
  private long startTime=SystemClock.uptimeMillis();
  private Handler handler=new Handler();
  private AtomicBoolean areWeDeadYet=new AtomicBoolean(false);

  @Override
  public void onCreate(Bundle icicle) {
    super.onCreate(icicle);
    setContentView(R.layout.main);
    getListView().addHeaderView(buildHeader());
    getListView().addFooterView(buildFooter());
    setListAdapter(new ArrayAdapter<String>(this,
                   android.R.layout.simple_list_item_1,
                   items));
  }

  @Override
  public void onDestroy() {
    super.onDestroy();

    areWeDeadYet.set(true);
  }

  private View buildHeader() {
    Button btn=new Button(this);
```

```java
    btn.setText("Randomize!");
    btn.setOnClickListener(new View.OnClickListener() {
      public void onClick(View v) {
        List<String> list=Arrays.asList(items);

        Collections.shuffle(list);

        setListAdapter(new ArrayAdapter<String>(HeaderFooterDemo.this,
                       android.R.layout.simple_list_item_1,
                       list));
      }
    });

    return(btn);
  }

  private View buildFooter() {
    TextView txt=new TextView(this);

    updateFooter(txt);

    return(txt);
  }

  private void updateFooter(final TextView txt) {
    long runtime=(SystemClock.uptimeMillis()-startTime)/1000;

    txt.setText(String.valueOf(runtime)+" seconds since activity launched");

    if (!areWeDeadYet.get()) {
      handler.postDelayed(new Runnable() {
        public void run() {

          updateFooter(txt);
        }
      }, 1000);
    }
  }
}
```

Here, we add a header `View` built via `buildHeader()`, returning a `Button` that, when clicked, will shuffle the contents of the list. We also add a footer `View` built via `buildFooter()`, returning a `TextView` that shows how long the activity has been running, updated every second. The list itself is the ever-popular list of *lorem ipsum* words.

When initially displayed, the header is visible but the footer is not, because the list is too long:

Figure 13. A ListView with a header view shown

If you scroll downward, the header will slide off the top, and eventually the footer will scroll into view:

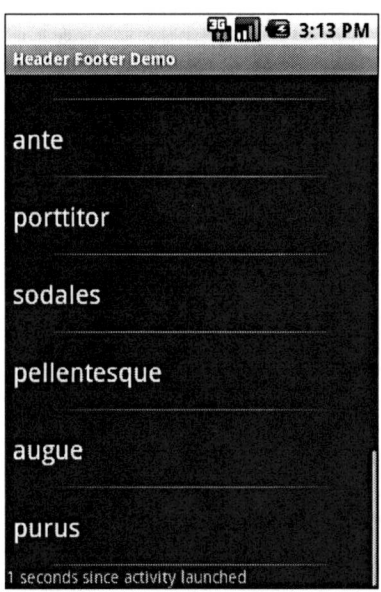

Figure 14. A ListView with a footer view shown

Control Your Selection

The stock Android UI for a selected `ListView` row is fairly simplistic: it highlights the row in orange...and nothing more. You can control the `Drawable` used for selection via the `android:listSelector` and `android:drawSelectorOnTop` attributes on the `ListView` element in your layout. However, even those simply apply some generic look to the selected row.

It may be you want to do something more elaborate for a selected row, such as changing the row around to expose more information. Maybe you have thumbnail photos but only display the photo on the selected row. Or perhaps you want to show some sort of secondary line of text, like a person's instant messenger status, only on the selected row. Or, there may be times you want a more subtle indication of the selected item than having the whole row show up in some neon color. The stock Android UI for highlighting a selection will not do any of this for you.

That just means you have to do it yourself. The good news is, it is not very difficult.

Create a Unified Row View

The simplest way to accomplish this is for each row `View` to have all of the widgets you want for the selected-row perspective, but with the "extra stuff" flagged as invisible at the outset. That way, rows initially look "normal" when put into the list – all you need to do is toggle the invisible widgets to visible when a row gets selected and toggle them back to invisible when a row is de-selected.

For example, in the `ListView/Selector` project, you will find a row.xml layout representing a row in a list:

```
<?xml version="1.0" encoding="utf-8"?>
<LinearLayout
  xmlns:android="http://schemas.android.com/apk/res/android"
  android:orientation="horizontal"
```

```
  android:layout_width="fill_parent"
  android:layout_height="fill_parent" >
<View
    android:id="@+id/bar"
    android:background="#FFFF0000"
    android:layout_width="5px"
    android:layout_height="fill_parent"
    android:visibility="invisible"
/>
<TextView
    android:id="@+id/label"
    android:layout_width="fill_parent"
    android:layout_height="fill_parent"
    android:textSize="10pt"
    android:paddingTop="2px"
    android:paddingBottom="2px"
    android:paddingLeft="5px"
/>
</LinearLayout>
```

There is a `TextView` representing the bulk of the row. Before it, though, on the left, is a plain `View` named `bar`. The background of the `View` is set to red (`android:background = "#FFFF0000"`) and the width to 5px. More importantly, it is set to be invisible (`android:visibility = "invisible"`). Hence, when the row is put into a `ListView`, the red bar is not seen...until we make the bar visible.

Configure the List, Get Control on Selection

Next, we need to set up a `ListView` and arrange to be notified when rows are selected and de-selected. That is merely a matter of calling `setOnItemSelectedListener()` for the `ListView`, providing a listener to be notified on a selection change. You can see that in the context of a `ListActivity` in our `SelectorDemo` class:

```
package com.commonsware.android.listview;

import android.app.ListActivity;
import android.content.Context;
import android.os.Bundle;
import android.content.res.ColorStateList;
import android.view.View;
import android.view.ViewGroup;
import android.widget.AdapterView;
import android.widget.ArrayAdapter;
import android.widget.ListView;
```

```java
import android.widget.TextView;

public class SelectorDemo extends ListActivity {
  private static ColorStateList allWhite=ColorStateList.valueOf(0xFFFFFFFF);
  private static String[] items={"lorem", "ipsum", "dolor",
                                 "sit", "amet", "consectetuer",
                                 "adipiscing", "elit", "morbi",
                                 "vel", "ligula", "vitae",
                                 "arcu", "aliquet", "mollis",
                                 "etiam", "vel", "erat",
                                 "placerat", "ante",
                                 "porttitor", "sodales",
                                 "pellentesque", "augue",
                                 "purus"};

  @Override
  public void onCreate(Bundle icicle) {
    super.onCreate(icicle);
    setContentView(R.layout.main);
    setListAdapter(new SelectorAdapter(this));
    getListView().setOnItemSelectedListener(listener);
  }

  class SelectorAdapter extends ArrayAdapter {
    SelectorAdapter(Context ctxt) {
      super(ctxt, R.layout.row, items);
    }

    @Override
    public View getView(int position, View convertView,
                        ViewGroup parent) {
      SelectorWrapper wrapper=null;

      if (convertView==null) {
        convertView=getLayoutInflater().inflate(R.layout.row,
                                                null);
        wrapper=new SelectorWrapper(convertView);
        wrapper.getLabel().setTextColor(allWhite);
        convertView.setTag(wrapper);
      }
      else {
        wrapper=(SelectorWrapper)convertView.getTag();
      }

      wrapper.getLabel().setText(items[position]);

      return(convertView);
    }
  }

  class SelectorWrapper {
    View row=null;
    TextView label=null;
    View bar=null;
```

```
    SelectorWrapper(View row) {
      this.row=row;
    }

    TextView getLabel() {
      if (label==null) {
        label=(TextView)row.findViewById(R.id.label);
      }

      return(label);
    }

    View getBar() {
      if (bar==null) {
        bar=row.findViewById(R.id.bar);
      }

      return(bar);
    }
  }

  AdapterView.OnItemSelectedListener listener=new
AdapterView.OnItemSelectedListener() {
    View lastRow=null;

    public void onItemSelected(AdapterView<?> parent,
                               View view, int position,
                               long id) {
      if (lastRow!=null) {
        SelectorWrapper wrapper=(SelectorWrapper)lastRow.getTag();

        wrapper.getBar().setVisibility(View.INVISIBLE);
      }

      SelectorWrapper wrapper=(SelectorWrapper)view.getTag();

      wrapper.getBar().setVisibility(View.VISIBLE);
      lastRow=view;
    }

    public void onNothingSelected(AdapterView<?> parent) {
      if (lastRow!=null) {
        SelectorWrapper wrapper=(SelectorWrapper)lastRow.getTag();

        wrapper.getBar().setVisibility(View.INVISIBLE);
        lastRow=null;
      }
    }
  };
}
```

`SelectorDemo` sets up a `SelectorAdapter`, which follow the view-wrapper pattern established in *The Busy Coder's Guide to Android Development*. Each row is created from the layout shown earlier, with a `SelectorWrapper` providing access to both the `TextView` (for setting the text in a row) and the bar `View`.

Change the Row

Our `AdapterView.OnItemSelectedListener` instance keeps track of the last selected row (`lastRow`). When the selection changes to another row in `onItemSelected()`, we make the bar from the last selected row invisible, before we make the bar visible on the newly-selected row. In `onNothingSelected()`, we make the bar invisible and make our last selected row be null.

The net effect is that as the selection changes, we toggle the bar off and on as needed to indicate which is the selected row.

In the layout for the activity's `ListView`, we turn off the regular highlighting:

```
<?xml version="1.0" encoding="utf-8"?>
<ListView
    xmlns:android="http://schemas.android.com/apk/res/android"
    android:id="@android:id/list"
    android:layout_width="fill_parent"
    android:layout_height="fill_parent"
    android:listSelector="#00000000"
/>
```

The result is we are controlling the highlight, in the form of the red bar:

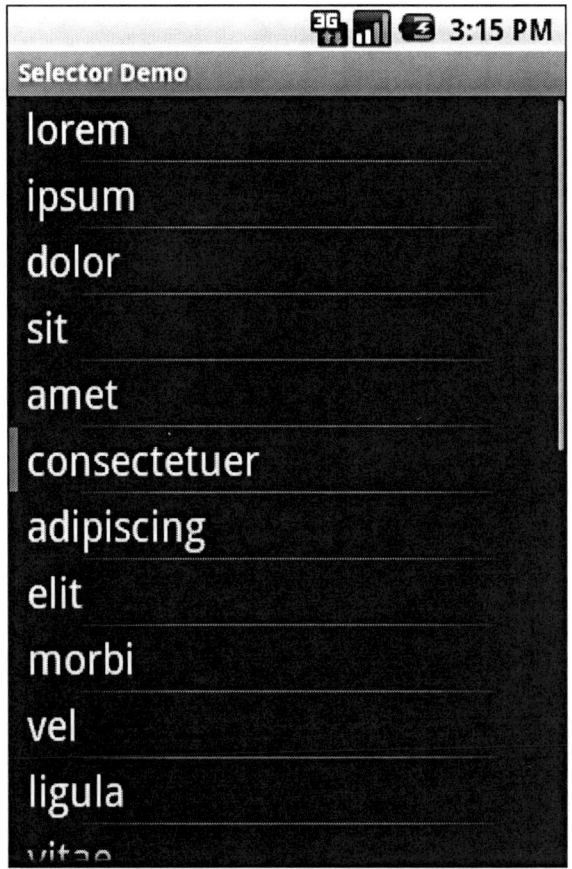

Figure 15. A ListView with a custom-drawn selector icon

Obviously, what we do to highlight a row could be much more elaborate than what is demonstrated here. At the same time, it needs to be fairly quick to execute, lest the list appear to be too sluggish.

CHAPTER 4

Show Up At Home

One of the oft-requested features added in Android 1.5 is the ability to add live elements to the home screen. Called "app widgets", these can be added by users via a long-tap on the home screen and choosing an appropriate widget from the available roster. Android ships with a few app widgets, such as a music player, but developers can add their own – in this chapter, we will see how this is done.

For the purposes of this book, "app widgets" will refer to these items that go on the home screen. Other uses of the term "widget" will be reserved for the UI widgets, subclasses of View, usually found in the android.widget Java package.

East is East, and West is West...

Part of the reason it took as long as it did for app widgets to become available is security.

Android's security model is based heavily on Linux user, file, and process security. Each application is (normally) associated with a unique user ID. All of its files are owned by that user, and its process(es) run as that user. This prevents one application from modifying the files of another or otherwise injecting their own code into another running process.

In particular, the core Android team wanted to find a way that would allow app widgets to be displayed by the home screen application, yet have their content come from another application. It would be dangerous for the home screen to run arbitrary code itself or somehow allow its UI to be directly manipulated by another process.

The app widget architecture, therefore, is set up to keep the home screen application independent from any code that puts app widgets on that home screen, so bugs in one cannot harm the other.

The Big Picture for a Small App Widget

The way Android pulls off this bit of security is through the use of `RemoteViews`.

The application component that supplies the UI for an app widget is not an `Activity`, but rather a `BroadcastReceiver` (often in tandem with a `Service`). The `BroadcastReceiver`, in turn, does not inflate a normal `View` hierarchy, like an `Activity` would, but instead inflates a layout into a `RemoteViews` object.

`RemoteViews` encapsulates a limited edition of normal widgets, in such a fashion that the `RemoteViews` can be "easily" transported across process boundaries. You configure the `RemoteViews` via your `BroadcastReceiver` and make those `RemoteViews` available to Android. Android in turn delivers the `RemoteViews` to the app widget host (usually the home screen), which renders them to the screen itself.

This architectural choice has many impacts:

1. You do not have access to the full range of widgets and containers. You can use `FrameLayout`, `LinearLayout`, and `RelativeLayout` for containers, and `AnalogClock`, `Button`, `Chronometer`, `ImageButton`, `ImageView`, `ProgressBar`, and `TextView` for widgets.

2. The only user input you can get is clicks of the `Button` and `ImageButton` widgets. In particular, there is no `EditText` for text input.

3. Because the app widgets are rendered in another process, you cannot simply register an `OnClickListener` to get button clicks; rather, you tell `RemoteViews` a `PendingIntent` to invoke when a given button is clicked.

4. You do not hold onto the `RemoteViews` and reuse them yourself. Rather, the pattern appears to be that you create and send out a brand-new `RemoteViews` whenever you want to change the contents of the app widget. This, coupled with having to transport the `RemoteViews` across process boundaries, means that updating the app widget is rather expensive in terms of CPU time, memory, and battery life.

5. Because the component handling the updates is a `BroadcastReceiver`, you have to be quick (lest you take too long and Android consider you to have timed out), you cannot use background threads, and your component itself is lost once the request has been completed. Hence, if your update might take a while, you will probably want to have the `BroadcastReceiver` start a `Service` and have the `Service` do the long-running task and eventual app widget update.

Crafting App Widgets

This will become somewhat easier to understand in the context of some sample code. In the `AppWidget/TwitterWidget` project, you will find an app widget that shows the latest tweet in your Twitter[18] timeline. If you have read *Android Programming Tutorials*, you will recognize the JTwitter JAR we will use for accessing the Twitter Web service.

---

18 http://twitter.com

The Manifest

First, we need to register our `BroadcastReceiver` (and, if relevant, `Service`) implementation in our `AndroidManifest.xml` file, along with a few extra features:

```xml
<?xml version="1.0" encoding="utf-8"?>
<manifest xmlns:android="http://schemas.android.com/apk/res/android"
    package="com.commonsware.android.appwidget"
    android:versionCode="1"
    android:versionName="1.0">
  <uses-permission android:name="android.permission.INTERNET" />
    <application android:label="@string/app_name">
        <activity android:name=".TWPrefs"
                  android:label="@string/app_name">
            <intent-filter>
                <action android:name="android.intent.action.MAIN" />
                <category android:name="android.intent.category.LAUNCHER" />
            </intent-filter>
            <intent-filter>
                <action
android:name="android.appwidget.action.APPWIDGET_CONFIGURE" />
            </intent-filter>
        </activity>
        <receiver android:name=".TwitterWidget"
            android:label="@string/app_name"
            android:icon="@drawable/tw_icon">
            <intent-filter>
                <action
                    android:name="android.appwidget.action.APPWIDGET_UPDATE" />
            </intent-filter>
            <meta-data
                android:name="android.appwidget.provider"
                android:resource="@xml/widget_provider" />
        </receiver>
        <service android:name=".TwitterWidget$UpdateService" />
    </application>
</manifest>
```

Here we have an `<activity>`, a `<receiver>`, and a `<service>`. Of note:

- Our `<receiver>` has `android:label` and `android:icon` attributes, which are not normally needed on `BroadcastReceiver` declarations. However, in this case, those are used for the entry that goes in the menu of available widgets to add to the home screen. Hence, you will probably want to supply values for both of those, and use appropriate resources in case you want translations for other languages.

- Our `<receiver>` has an `<intent-filter>` for the `android.appwidget.action.APPWIDGET_UPDATE` action. This means we will get control whenever Android wants us to update the content of our app widget. There may be other actions we want to monitor – more on this in a later section.

- Our `<receiver>` also has a `<meta-data>` element, indicating that its `android.appwidget.provider` details can be found in the `res/xml/widget_provider.xml` file. This metadata is described in the next section.

- Our `<activity>` has two `<intent-filter>` elements, the normal "put me in the Launcher" one and one looking for an action of `android.appwidget.action.APPWIDGET_CONFIGURE`.

The Metadata

Next, we need to define the app widget provider metadata. This has to reside at the location indicated in the manifest – in this case, in `res/xml/widget_provider.xml`:

```
<appwidget-provider xmlns:android="http://schemas.android.com/apk/res/android"
  android:minWidth="292dip"
  android:minHeight="72dip"
  android:updatePeriodMillis="900000"
  android:configure="com.commonsware.android.appwidget.TWPrefs"
/>
```

Here, we provide four pieces of information:

- The minimum width and height of the app widget (`android:minWidth` and `android:minHeight`). These are approximate – the app widget host (e.g., home screen) will tend to convert these values into "cells" based upon the overall layout of the UI where the app widgets will reside. However, they should be no smaller than the minimums cited here.

- The frequency in which Android should request an update of the widget's contents (`android:updatePeriodMillis`). This is expressed in terms of milliseconds, so a value of `900000` is a 15-minute update cycle.

- An activity class that will be used to configure the widget when it is first added to the screen (`android:configure`). This will be described in greater detail in a later section.

The configuration activity is optional. However, if you skip the configuration activity, you do need to tell Android the initial layout to use for the app widget, via an `android:initialLayout` attribute.

The Layout

Eventually, you are going to need a layout that describes what the app widget looks like. So long as you stick to the widget and container classes noted above, this layout can otherwise look like any other layout in your project.

For example, here is the layout for the `TwitterWidget`:

```xml
<?xml version="1.0" encoding="utf-8"?>
<RelativeLayout xmlns:android="http://schemas.android.com/apk/res/android"
    android:orientation="horizontal"
    android:layout_width="fill_parent"
    android:layout_height="fill_parent"
    android:background="#FF000088"
    >
  <ImageButton android:id="@+id/refresh"
    android:layout_alignParentTop="true"
    android:layout_alignParentRight="true"
    android:src="@drawable/refresh"
    android:layout_width="wrap_content"
    android:layout_height="wrap_content"
  />
  <ImageButton android:id="@+id/configure"
    android:layout_alignParentBottom="true"
    android:layout_alignParentRight="true"
    android:src="@drawable/configure"
    android:layout_width="wrap_content"
    android:layout_height="wrap_content"
  />
  <TextView android:id="@+id/friend"
    android:layout_alignParentTop="true"
    android:layout_alignParentLeft="true"
    android:layout_toLeftOf="@id/refresh"
    android:layout_width="wrap_content"
    android:layout_height="wrap_content"
    android:gravity="left"
```

```
    android:textStyle="bold"
    android:singleLine="true"
    android:ellipsize="end"
  />
  <TextView android:id="@+id/status"
    android:layout_below="@id/friend"
    android:layout_alignParentLeft="true"
    android:layout_toLeftOf="@id/refresh"
    android:layout_width="wrap_content"
    android:layout_height="fill_parent"
    android:gravity="top"
    android:singleLine="false"
    android:lines="4"
  />
</RelativeLayout>
```

All we have is a `TextView` to show the latest tweet, plus another one for the person issuing the tweet, and a pair of `ImageButton` widgets to allow the user to manually refresh the latest tweet and launch the configuration activity.

The BroadcastReceiver

Next, we need a `BroadcastReciever` that can get control when Android wants us to update our `RemoteViews` for our app widget. To simplify this, Android supplies an `AppWidgetProvider` class we can extend, instead of the normal `BroadcastReceiver`. This simply looks at the received `Intent` and calls out to an appropriate lifecycle method based on the requested action.

The one method that invariably needs to be implemented on the provider is `onUpdate()`. Other lifecycle methods may be of interest and are discussed later in this chapter.

For example, here is the `onUpdate()` implementation of the `AppWidgetProvider` for `TwitterWidget`:

```
@Override
public void onUpdate(Context ctxt,
                     AppWidgetManager mgr,
                     int[] appWidgetIds) {
  ctxt.startService(new Intent(ctxt, UpdateService.class));
}
```

If our `RemoteViews` could be rapidly constructed, we could do the work right here. However, in our case, we need to make a Web service call to Twitter, which might take a while, so we instead call `startService()` on the `Service` we declared in our manifest, to have it make the updates.

The Service

The real work for `TwitterWidget` is mostly done in an `UpdateService` inner class of `TwitterWidget`.

`UpdateService` does not extend `Service`, but rather extends `IntentService`. `IntentService` is designed for patterns like this one, where our service is started multiple times, with each "start" representing a distinct piece of work to be accomplished (in this case, updating an app widget from Twitter). `IntentService` allows us to implement `onHandleIntent()` to do this work, and it arranges for `onHandleIntent()` to be called on a background thread. Hence, we do not need to deal with starting or stopping our thread, or even stopping our service when there is no more work to be done – Android handles that automatically.

Here is the `onHandleIntent()` implementation from `UpdateService`:

```
@Override
public void onHandleIntent(Intent intent) {
  ComponentName me=new ComponentName(this,
                                     TwitterWidget.class);
  AppWidgetManager mgr=AppWidgetManager.getInstance(this);

  mgr.updateAppWidget(me, buildUpdate(this));
}
```

To update the `RemoteViews` for our app widget, we need to build those `RemoteViews` (delegated to a `buildUpdate()` helper method) and tell an `AppWidgetManager` to update the widget via `updateAppWidget()`. In this case, we use a version of `updateAppWidget()` that takes a `ComponentName` as the identifier of the widget to be updated. Note that this means that we will update all instances of this app widget presently in use – the concept of multiple app widget instances is covered in greater detail later in this chapter.

Working with `RemoteViews` is a bit like trying to tie your shoes while wearing mittens – it may be possible, but it is a bit clumsy. In this case, rather than using methods like `findViewById()` and then calling methods on individual widgets, we need to call methods on `RemoteViews` itself, providing the identifier of the widget we wish to modify. This is so our requests for changes can be serialized for transport to the home screen process. It does, however, mean that our view-updating code looks a fair bit different than it would if this were the main `View` of an activity or row of a `ListView`.

For example, here is the `buildUpdate()` method from `UpdateService`, which builds a `RemoteViews` containing the latest Twitter information, using account information pulled from shared preferences:

```java
private RemoteViews buildUpdate(Context context) {
  RemoteViews updateViews=new RemoteViews(context.getPackageName(),
                                      R.layout.widget);
  String user=prefs.getString("user", null);
  String password=prefs.getString("password", null);

  if (user!=null && password!=null) {
    Twitter client=new Twitter(user, password);
    List<Twitter.Status> timeline=client.getFriendsTimeline();

    if (timeline.size()>0) {
      Twitter.Status s=timeline.get(0);

      updateViews.setTextViewText(R.id.friend,
                                  s.user.screenName);
      updateViews.setTextViewText(R.id.status,
                                  s.text);

      Intent i=new Intent(this, TwitterWidget.class);
      PendingIntent pi=PendingIntent.getBroadcast(context,
                                                 0 , i,
                                                 0);

      updateViews.setOnClickPendingIntent(R.id.refresh,
                                          pi);

      i=new Intent(this, TWPrefs.class);
      pi=PendingIntent.getActivity(context, 0 , i, 0);
      updateViews.setOnClickPendingIntent(R.id.configure,
                                          pi);
    }
  }

  return(updateViews);
}
```

To create the `RemoteViews`, we use a constructor that takes our package name and the identifier of our layout. This gives us a `RemoteViews` that contains all of the widgets we declared in that layout, just as if we inflated the layout using a `LayoutInflater`. The difference, of course, is that we have a `RemoteViews` object, not a `View`, as the result.

We then use methods like:

- `setTextViewText()` to set the text on a `TextView` in the `RemoteViews`, given the identifier of the `TextView` within the layout we wish to manipulate
- `setOnClickPendingIntent()` to provide a `PendingIntent` that should get fired off when a `Button` or `ImageButton` is clicked

Note, of course, that Android does not know anything about Twitter – the Twitter object comes from a JTwitter JAR located in the `libs/` directory of our project.

The Configuration Activity

Way back in the manifest, we included an `<activity>` element for a `TWPrefs` activity. And, in our widget metadata XML file, we said that `TWPrefs` was the `android:configure` attribute value. In our `RemoteViews` for the widget itself, we connect a configure button to launch `TWPrefs` when clicked.

The net of all of this is that `TWPrefs` is the configuration activity. Specifically:

- It will be launched when we request to add this widget to our home screen
- It will be re-launched whenever we click the configure button in the widget itself

For the latter scenario, the activity need be nothing special. In fact, `TWPrefs` is mostly just a `PreferenceActivity`, updating the `SharedPreferences` for this application with the user's Twitter screen name and password, used for logging into Twitter and fetching the latest timeline entry.

The former scenario – defining a configuration activity in the metadata – requires a bit more work, though.

If we were to leave this out, and not have an android:configure attribute in the metadata, once the user chose to add our widget to their home screen, the widget would immediately appear. Behind the scenes, Android would ask our AppWidgetProvider to supply the RemoteViews for the widget body right away.

However, when we declare that we want a configuration activity, we must build the initial RemoteViews ourselves and return them as the activity's result. Behind the scenes, Android uses startActivityForResult() to launch our configuration activity, then looks at the result and uses the associated RemoteViews to create the initial look of the widget.

This approach is prone to code duplication, and it is not completely clear why Android elected to build the widget framework this way.

That being said, here is the implementation of TWPrefs:

```java
package com.commonsware.android.appwidget;

import android.app.Activity;
import android.appwidget.AppWidgetManager;
import android.appwidget.AppWidgetProvider;
import android.content.ComponentName;
import android.content.Intent;
import android.os.Bundle;
import android.preference.PreferenceActivity;
import android.view.KeyEvent;
import android.widget.RemoteViews;

public class TWPrefs extends PreferenceActivity {
  private static String CONFIGURE_ACTION="android.appwidget.action.APPWIDGET_CONFIGURE";

  @Override
  public void onCreate(Bundle savedInstanceState) {
    super.onCreate(savedInstanceState);

    addPreferencesFromResource(R.xml.preferences);
  }

  @Override
```

```java
public boolean onKeyDown(int keyCode, KeyEvent event) {
  if (keyCode==KeyEvent.KEYCODE_BACK) {
    if (CONFIGURE_ACTION.equals(getIntent().getAction())) {
      Intent intent=getIntent();
      Bundle extras=intent.getExtras();

      if (extras!=null) {
        int id=extras.getInt(AppWidgetManager.EXTRA_APPWIDGET_ID,
                             AppWidgetManager.INVALID_APPWIDGET_ID);
        AppWidgetManager mgr=AppWidgetManager.getInstance(this);
        RemoteViews views=new RemoteViews(getPackageName(),
                                          R.layout.widget);

        mgr.updateAppWidget(id, views);

        Intent result=new Intent();

        result.putExtra(AppWidgetManager.EXTRA_APPWIDGET_ID,
                        id);
        setResult(RESULT_OK, result);
        sendBroadcast(new Intent(this,
                                 TwitterWidget.class));
      }
    }
  }

  return(super.onKeyDown(keyCode, event));
}
```

We are using the same activity for two cases: for the initial configuration and for later on-demand reconfiguration via the configure button in the widget. We need to tell these apart. More importantly, we need to get control at an appropriate time to set our activity result in the initial configuration case. Alas, the normal activity lifecycle methods (e.g., onDestroy()) are too late, and PreferenceActivity offers no other explicit hook to find out when the user dismisses the preference screen.

So, we have to cheat a bit.

Specifically, we hook onKeyDown() and watch for the back button. When the back button is pressed, if we were launched by a widget configuration Intent (CONFIGURE_ACTION.equals(getIntent().getAction())), then we go through and:

- Get our widget instance identifier (described in greater detail later in this chapter)
- Get our `AppWidgetManager` and create a new `RemoteViews` inflated from our widget layout
- Pass the empty `RemoteViews` to the `AppWidgetManager` via `updateAppWidget()`
- Call `setResult()` with an `Intent` wrapping our widget instance identifier, so Android knows we have properly configured our widget
- Raise a broadcast `Intent` to ask our `WidgetProvider` to do the *real* initial version of the widget

This minimizes code duplication, but it does mean there is a slight hiccup, where the widget initially appears blank, before the first timeline entry appears. This is largely unavoidable in this case – we cannot wait for Twitter to respond since `onKeyDown()` is called on the UI thread and we need to call `setResult()` now rather than wait for Twitter's response.

Undoubtedly, there are other patterns for handling this situation.

The Result

If you compile and install all of this, you will have a new widget entry available when you long-tap on the home screen background:

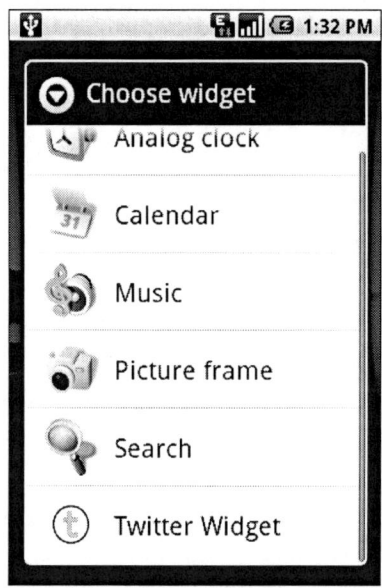

Figure 16. The roster of available widgets

When you choose Twitter Widget, you will initially be presented with the configuration activity:

Figure 17. The TwitterWidget configuration activity

Once you set your Twitter screen name and password, and press the back button to exit the activity, your widget will appear with no contents:

Figure 18. TwitterWidget, immediately after being added

After a moment, though, it will appear with the latest in your Twitter friends timeline:

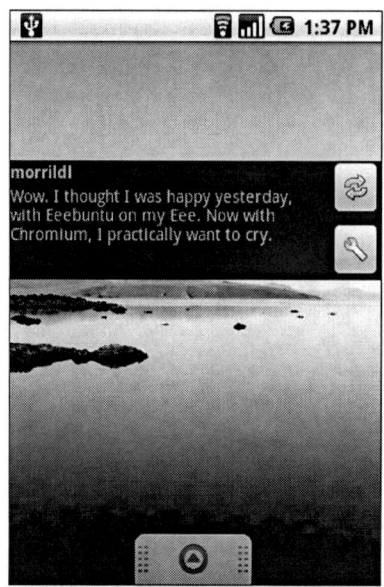

Figure 19. TwitterWidget, with a timeline entry

To change your Twitter credentials, you can either tap the configure icon in the widget or run the Twitter Widget application in your launcher. And, clicking the refresh button, or waiting 15 minutes, will cause the widget to update its contents.

Another and Another

As indicated above, you can have multiple instances of the same app widget outstanding at any one time. For example, one might have multiple picture frames, or multiple "show-me-the-latest-RSS-entry" app widgets, one per feed. You will distinguish between these in your code via the identifier supplied in the relevant AppWidgetProvider callbacks (e.g., onUpdate()).

If you want to support separate app widget instances, you will need to store your state on a per-app-widget-identifier basis. For example, while TwitterWidget uses preferences for the Twitter account details, you might need multiple preference files, or use a SQLite database with an app widget identifier column, or something to distinguish one app widget instance from another. You will also need to use an appropriate version of `updateAppWidget()` on `AppWidgetManager` when you update the app widgets, one that takes app widget identifiers as the first parameter, so you update the proper app widget instances.

Conversely, there is nothing requiring you to support multiple instances as independent entities. For example, if you add more than one `TwitterWidget` to your home screen, nothing blows up – they just show the same tweet. In the case of `TwitterWidget`, they might not even show the same tweet all the time, since they will update on independent cycles, so one will get newer tweets before another.

App Widgets: Their Life and Times

TwitterWidget overrode two `AppWidgetProvider` methods:

- `onUpdate()`, invoked when the `android:updatePeriodMillis` time has elapsed
- `onReceive()`, the standard `BroadcastReceiver` callback, used to detect when we are invoked with no action, meaning we want to force an update due to the refresh button being clicked

There are three other lifecycle methods that `AppWidgetProvider` offers that you may be interested in:

- `onEnabled()` will be called when the first widget instance is created for this particular widget provider, so if there is anything you need to do once for all supported widgets, you can implement that logic here
- `onDeleted()` will be called when a widget instance is removed from the home screen, in case there is any data you need to clean up specific to that instance
- `onDisabled()` will be called when the last widget instance for this provider is removed from the home screen, so you can clean up anything related to all such widgets

Note, however, that there is a bug in Android 1.5r2, where `onDeleted()` will not be properly called. You will need to implement `onReceive()` and watch for the `ACTION_APPWIDGET_DELETED` action in the received `Intent` and call `onDeleted()` yourself. This should be fixed in a future edition of Android.

Controlling Your (App Widget's) Destiny

As `TwitterWidget` illustrates, you are not limited to updating your app widget only based on the timetable specified in your metadata. That timetable is useful if you can get by with a fixed schedule. However, there are cases in which that will not work very well:

- If you want the user to be able to configure the polling period (the metadata is baked into your APK and therefore cannot be modified at runtime)
- If you want the app widget to be updated based on external factors, such as a change in location

The recipe shown in `TwitterWidget` will let you use `AlarmManager` (described in a later chapter) or proximity alerts or whatever to trigger updates. All you need to do is:

- Arrange for something to broadcast an `Intent` that will be picked up by the `BroadcastReceiver` you are using for your app widget provider
- Have the provider process that `Intent` directly or pass it along to a `Service` (such as an `IntentService` as shown in `TwitterWidget`)

Being a Good Host

In addition to creating your own app widgets, it is possible to host app widgets. This is mostly aimed for those creating alternative home screen applications, so they can take advantage of the same app widget framework and all the app widgets being built for it.

This is not very well documented at this juncture, but it apparently involves the `AppWidgetHost` and `AppWidgetHostView` classes. The latter is a `View` and so should be able to reside in an app widget host's UI like any other ordinary widget.

PART II – Advanced Media

CHAPTER 5

Creating Drawables

Drawable resources come in all shapes and sizes, and not just in terms of pixel dimensions. While many Drawable resources will be PNG or JPEG files, you can easily create other resources that supply other sorts of Drawable objects to your application. In this chapter, we will examine a few of these that may prove useful as you try to make your application look its best.

Traversing Along a Gradient

Gradients have long been used to add "something a little extra" to a user interface, whether it is Microsoft adding them to Office's title bars in the late 1990's or the seemingly endless number of gradient buttons adorning "Web 2.0" sites.

And now, you can have gradients in your Android applications as well.

The easiest way to create a gradient is to use an XML file to describe the gradient. By placing the file in res/drawable/, it can be referenced as a Drawable resource, no different than any other such resource, like a PNG file.

For example, here is a gradient Drawable resource, active_row.xml, from the Drawable/Gradient sample project:

Creating Drawables

```xml
<shape xmlns:android="http://schemas.android.com/apk/res/android"
  android:shape="rectangle">
  <gradient
    android:startColor="#44FF0000"
    android:endColor="#FFFF0000"
    android:angle="270"
  />
  <padding
    android:top="2px"
    android:bottom="2px"
  />
  <corners android:radius="6px" />
</shape>
```

A gradient is applied to the more general-purpose `<shape>` element, in this case, a rectangle. The gradient is defined as having a start and end color – in this case, the gradient is an increasing amount of red, with only the alpha channel varying to control how much the background blends in. The color is applied in a direction determined by the number of degrees specified by the `android:angle` attribute, with `270` representing "down" (start color at the top, end color at the bottom).

As with any other XML-defined shape, you can control various aspects of the way the shape is drawn. In this case, we put some padding around the drawable and round off the corners of the rectangle.

To use this `Drawable` in Java code, you can reference it as `R.drawable.active_row`. One possible use of a gradient is in custom `ListView` row selection, as shown in `Drawable/GradientDemo`:

```java
package com.commonsware.android.drawable;

import android.app.ListActivity;
import android.content.Context;
import android.os.Bundle;
import android.content.res.ColorStateList;
import android.view.View;
import android.view.ViewGroup;
import android.widget.AdapterView;
import android.widget.ArrayAdapter;
import android.widget.ListView;
import android.widget.TextView;

public class GradientDemo extends ListActivity {
  private static ColorStateList allWhite=ColorStateList.valueOf(0xFFFFFFFF);
  private static String[] items={"lorem", "ipsum", "dolor",
```

Creating Drawables

```java
                           "sit", "amet", "consectetuer",
                           "adipiscing", "elit", "morbi",
                           "vel", "ligula", "vitae",
                           "arcu", "aliquet", "mollis",
                           "etiam", "vel", "erat",
                           "placerat", "ante",
                           "porttitor", "sodales",
                           "pellentesque", "augue",
                           "purus"};

  @Override
  public void onCreate(Bundle icicle) {
    super.onCreate(icicle);
    setContentView(R.layout.main);
    setListAdapter(new GradientAdapter(this));
    getListView().setOnItemSelectedListener(listener);
  }

  class GradientAdapter extends ArrayAdapter {
    GradientAdapter(Context ctxt) {
      super(ctxt, R.layout.row, items);
    }

    @Override
    public View getView(int position, View convertView,
                        ViewGroup parent) {
      GradientWrapper wrapper=null;

      if (convertView==null) {
        convertView=getLayoutInflater().inflate(R.layout.row,
                                                null);
        wrapper=new GradientWrapper(convertView);
        convertView.setTag(wrapper);
      }
      else {
        wrapper=(GradientWrapper)convertView.getTag();
      }

      wrapper.getLabel().setText(items[position]);

      return(convertView);
    }
  }

  class GradientWrapper {
    View row=null;
    TextView label=null;

    GradientWrapper(View row) {
      this.row=row;
    }

    TextView getLabel() {
      if (label==null) {
```

```
      label=(TextView)row.findViewById(R.id.label);
    }

    return(label);
  }
}

AdapterView.OnItemSelectedListener listener=new
AdapterView.OnItemSelectedListener() {
  View lastRow=null;

  public void onItemSelected(AdapterView<?> parent,
                             View view, int position,
                             long id) {
    if (lastRow!=null) {
      lastRow.setBackgroundColor(0x00000000);
    }

    view.setBackgroundResource(R.drawable.active_row);
    lastRow=view;
  }

  public void onNothingSelected(AdapterView<?> parent) {
    if (lastRow!=null) {
      lastRow.setBackgroundColor(0x00000000);
      lastRow=null;
    }
  }
};
}
```

In an earlier chapter, we showed how you can get control and customize how a selected row appears in a ListView. This time, we apply the gradient rounded rectangle as the background of the row. We could have accomplished this via appropriate choices for android:listSelector and android:drawSelectorOnTop as well.

The result is a selection bar implementing the gradient:

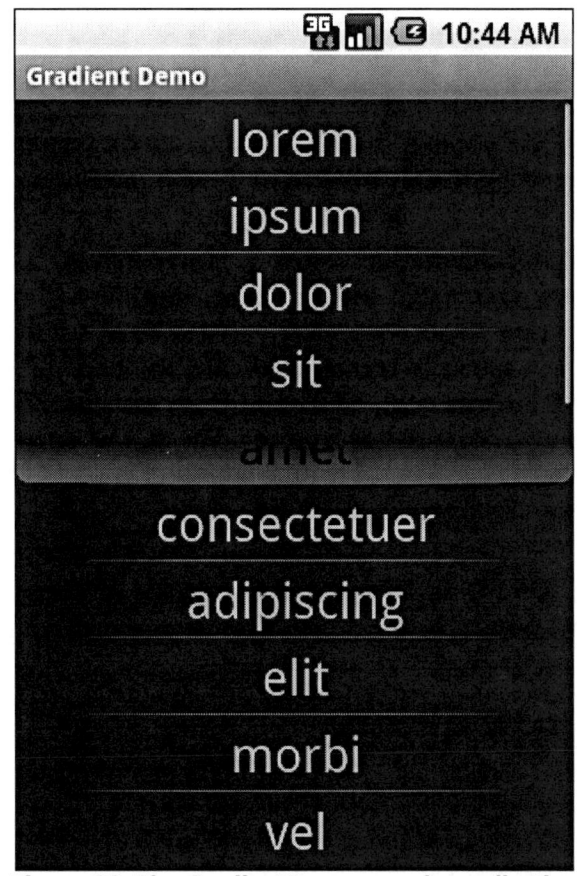

Figure 20. The GradientDemo sample application

Note that because the list background is black, the red is mixed with black on the top end of the gradient. If the list background were white, the top end of the gradient would be red mixed with white, as determined by the alpha channel specified on the gradient's top color.

A Stitch In Time Saves Nine

As you read through the Android documentation, you no doubt ran into references to "nine-patch" or "9-patch" and wondered what Android had to do with quilting[19]. Rest assured, you will not need to take up needlework to be an effective Android developer.

If, however, you are looking to create backgrounds for resizable widgets, like a Button, you will probably need to work with nine-patch images.

As the Android documentation states, a nine-patch is "a PNG image in which you define stretchable sections that Android will resize to fit the object at display time to accommodate variable sized sections, such as text strings". By using a specially-created PNG file, Android can avoid trying to use vector-based formats (e.g., SVG) and their associated overhead when trying to create a background at runtime. Yet, at the same time, Android can still resize the background to handle whatever you want to put inside of it, such as the text of a Button.

In this section, we will cover some of the basics of nine-patch graphics, including how to customize and apply them to your own Android layouts.

The Name and the Border

Nine-patch graphics are PNG files whose names end in .9.png. This means they can be edited using normal graphics tools, but Android knows to apply nine-patch rules to their use.

What makes a nine-patch graphic different than an ordinary PNG is a one-pixel-wide border surrounding the image. When drawn, Android will remove that border, showing only the stretched rendition of what lies inside the border. The border is used as a control channel, providing instructions to Android for how to deal with stretching the image to fit its contents.

---

19 http://www.qnm.com/articles/feature64/

Padding and the Box

Along the right and bottom sides, you can draw one-pixel-wide black lines to indicate the "padding box". Android will stretch the image such that the contents of the widget will fit inside that padding box.

For example, suppose we are using a nine-patch as the background of a Button. When you set the text to appear in the button (e.g., "Hello, world!"), Android will compute the size of that text, in terms of width and height in pixels. Then, it will stretch the nine-patch image such that the text will reside inside the padding box. What lies outside the padding box forms the border of the button, typically a rounded rectangle of some form.

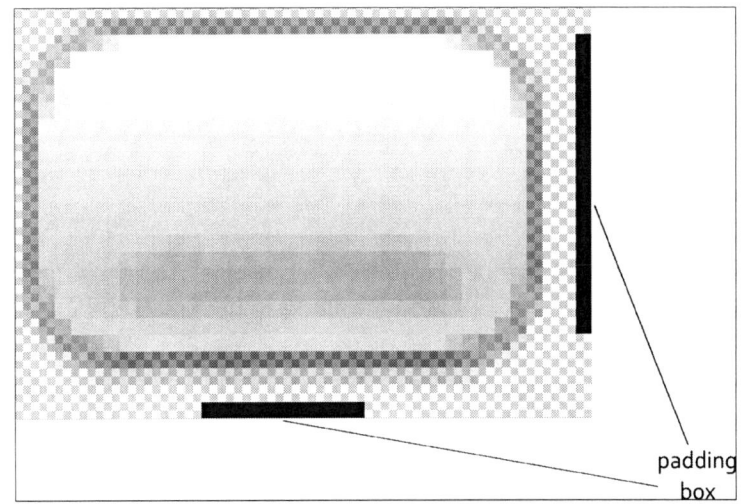

Figure 21. The padding box, as shown by a set of control lines to the right and bottom of the stretchable image

Stretch Zones

To tell Android where on the image to actually do the stretching, draw one-pixel-wide black lines on the top and left sides of the image. Android will scale the graphic only in those areas – areas outside the stretch zones are not stretched.

Creating Drawables

Perhaps the most common pattern is the center-stretch, where the middle portions of the image on both axes are considered stretchable, but the edges are not:

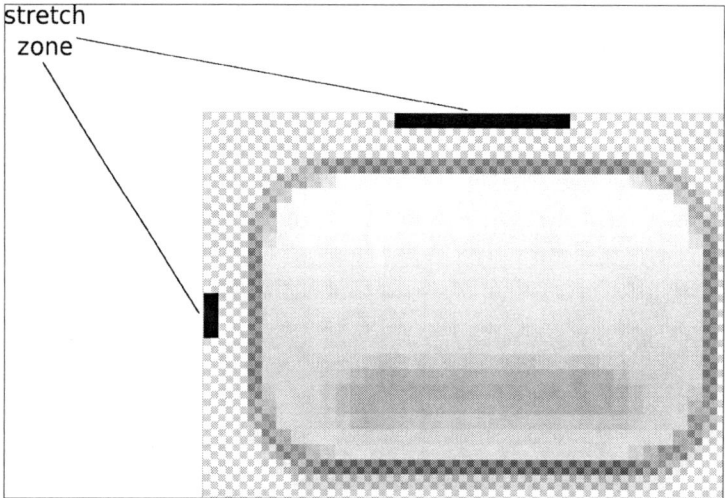

Figure 22. The stretch zones, as shown by a set of control lines to the right and bottom of the stretchable image

Here, the stretch zones will be stretched just enough for the contents to fit in the padding box. The edges of the graphic are left unstretched.

Some additional rules to bear in mind:

- If you have multiple discrete stretch zones along an axis (e.g., two zones separated by whitespace), Android will stretch both of them but keep them in their current proportions. So, if the first zone is twice as wide as the second zone in the original graphic, the first zone will be twice as wide as the second zone in the stretched graphic.
- If you leave out the control lines for the padding box, it is assumed that the padding box and the stretch zones are one and the same.

Tooling

To experiment with nine-patch images, you may wish to use the `draw9patch` program, found in the `tools/` directory of your SDK installation:

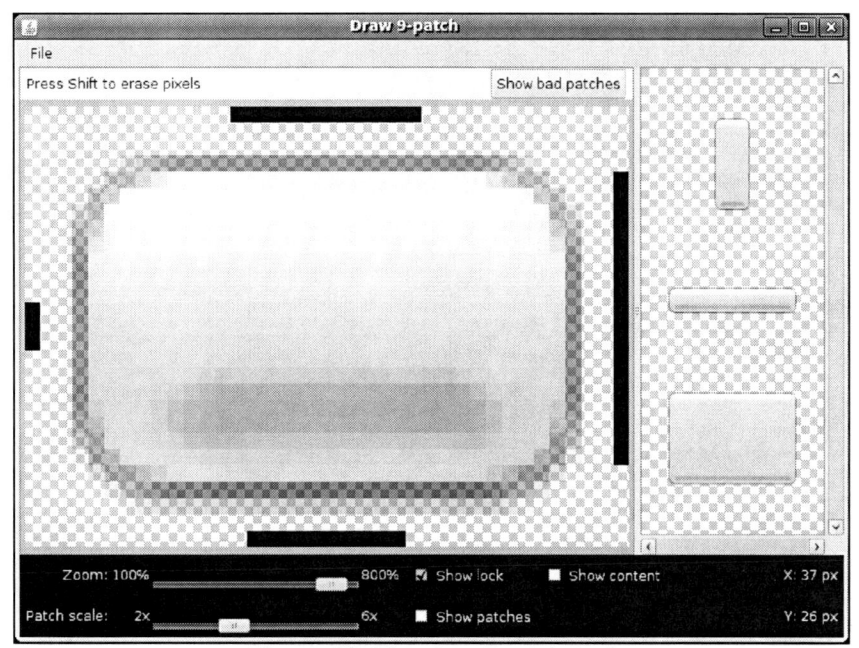

Figure 23. The draw9patch tool

While a regular graphics editor would allow you to draw any color on any pixel, `draw9patch` limits you to drawing or erasing pixels in the control area. If you attempt to draw inside the main image area itself, you will be blocked.

On the right, you will see samples of the image in various stretched sizes, so you can see the impact as you change the stretchable zones and padding box.

While this is convenient for working with the nine-patch nature of the image, you will still need some other graphics editor to create or modify the body of the image itself. For example, the image shown above, from the `Drawable/NinePatch` project, is a modified version of a nine-patch graphic from the SDK's `ApiDemos`, where the GIMP was used to add the neon green stripe across the bottom portion of the image.

Using Nine-Patch Images

Nine-patch images are most commonly used as backgrounds, as illustrated by the following layout:

```xml
<?xml version="1.0" encoding="utf-8"?>
<LinearLayout xmlns:android="http://schemas.android.com/apk/res/android"
  android:orientation="vertical"
  android:layout_width="fill_parent"
  android:layout_height="fill_parent"
  >
<TableLayout
    android:layout_width="fill_parent"
    android:layout_height="wrap_content"
    android:stretchColumns="1"
    >
  <TableRow
      android:layout_width="fill_parent"
      android:layout_height="wrap_content"
    >
    <TextView
        android:layout_width="wrap_content"
        android:layout_height="wrap_content"
        android:layout_gravity="center_vertical"
        android:text="Horizontal:"
    />
    <SeekBar android:id="@+id/horizontal"
        android:layout_width="fill_parent"
        android:layout_height="wrap_content"
    />
  </TableRow>
  <TableRow
      android:layout_width="fill_parent"
      android:layout_height="wrap_content"
    >
    <TextView
        android:layout_width="wrap_content"
        android:layout_height="wrap_content"
        android:layout_gravity="center_vertical"
        android:text="Vertical:"
    />
    <SeekBar android:id="@+id/vertical"
        android:layout_width="fill_parent"
        android:layout_height="wrap_content"
    />
  </TableRow>
</TableLayout>
```

```
  <LinearLayout
    android:orientation="vertical"
    android:layout_width="fill_parent"
    android:layout_height="fill_parent"
    >
    <Button android:id="@+id/resize"
      android:layout_width="48px"
      android:layout_height="48px"
      android:text="Hi!"
      android:background="@drawable/button"
    />
  </LinearLayout>
</LinearLayout>
```

Here, we have two `SeekBar` widgets, labeled for the horizontal and vertical axes, plus a `Button` set up with our nine-patch graphic as its background (`android:background = "@drawable/button"`).

The `NinePatchDemo` activity then uses the two `SeekBar` widgets to let the user control how large the button should be drawn on-screen, starting from an initial size of 48px square:

```
package com.commonsware.android.drawable;

import android.app.Activity;
import android.os.Bundle;
import android.view.View;
import android.view.ViewGroup;
import android.widget.LinearLayout;
import android.widget.SeekBar;

public class NinePatchDemo extends Activity {
  SeekBar horizontal=null;
  SeekBar vertical=null;
  View thingToResize=null;

  @Override
  public void onCreate(Bundle savedInstanceState) {
    super.onCreate(savedInstanceState);
    setContentView(R.layout.main);

    thingToResize=findViewById(R.id.resize);

    horizontal=(SeekBar)findViewById(R.id.horizontal);
    vertical=(SeekBar)findViewById(R.id.vertical);

    horizontal.setMax(272);   // 320 less 48 starting size
    vertical.setMax(272);     // keep it square @ max

    horizontal.setOnSeekBarChangeListener(h);
```

Creating Drawables

```java
      vertical.setOnSeekBarChangeListener(v);
  }

  SeekBar.OnSeekBarChangeListener h=new SeekBar.OnSeekBarChangeListener() {
    public void onProgressChanged(SeekBar seekBar,
                                  int progress,
                                  boolean fromTouch) {
      ViewGroup.LayoutParams old=thingToResize.getLayoutParams();
      ViewGroup.LayoutParams current=new LinearLayout.LayoutParams(48+progress,
                                                                    old.height);

      thingToResize.setLayoutParams(current);
    }

    public void onStartTrackingTouch(SeekBar seekBar) {
      // unused
    }

    public void onStopTrackingTouch(SeekBar seekBar) {
      // unused
    }
  };

  SeekBar.OnSeekBarChangeListener v=new SeekBar.OnSeekBarChangeListener() {
    public void onProgressChanged(SeekBar seekBar,
                                  int progress,
                                  boolean fromTouch) {
      ViewGroup.LayoutParams old=thingToResize.getLayoutParams();
      ViewGroup.LayoutParams current=new LinearLayout.LayoutParams(old.width,
                                                                    48+progress);

      thingToResize.setLayoutParams(current);
    }

    public void onStartTrackingTouch(SeekBar seekBar) {
      // unused
    }

    public void onStopTrackingTouch(SeekBar seekBar) {
      // unused
    }
  };
}
```

The result is an application that can be used much like the right pane of draw9patch, to see how the nine-patch graphic looks on an actual device or emulator in various sizes:

Figure 25. The NinePatch sample project, in its initial state

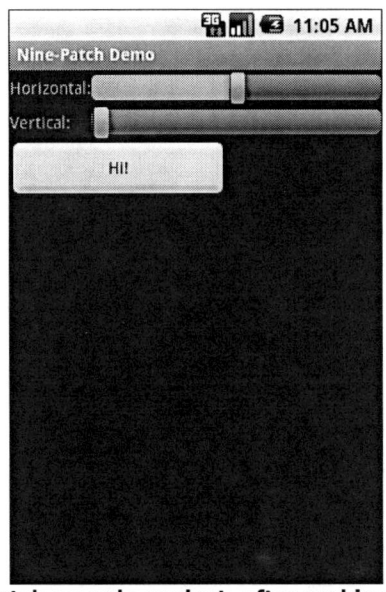

Figure 26. The NinePatch sample project, after making it bigger horizontally

Creating Drawables

Figure 27. The NinePatch sample application, after making it bigger in both dimensions

CHAPTER 6

Animating Widgets

Android is full of things that move. You can swipe left and right on the home screen to view other panels of the desktop. You can drag icons around on the home screen. You can drag down the notifications area or drag up the applications drawer. And that is just on one screen!

Of course, it would be nice to employ such animations in your own application. While this chapter will not cover full-fledged drag-and-drop, we will cover some of the basic animations and how to apply them to your existing widgets.

It's Not Just For Toons Anymore

Android has a package of classes (android.view.animation) dedicated to animating the movement and behavior of widgets.

They center around an Animation base class that describes what is to be done. Built-in animations exist to move a widget (TranslateAnimation), change the transparency of a widget (AlphaAnimation), revolving a widget (RotateAnimation), and resizing a widget (ScaleAnimation). There is even a way to aggregate animations together into a composite Animation called an AnimationSet. Later sections in this chapter will examine the use of several of these animations.

Given that you have an animation, to apply it, you have two main options:

Animating Widgets

- You may be using a container that supports animating its contents, such as a `ViewFlipper` or `TextSwitcher`. These are typically subclasses of `ViewAnimator` and let you define the "in" and "out" animations to apply. For example, with a `ViewFlipper`, you can specify how it flips between `Views` in terms of what animation is used to animate "out" the currently-visible `View` and what animation is used to animate "in" the replacement `View`. Examples of this sort of animation can be found in *The Busy Coder's Guide to Android Development*.

- You can simply tell any `View` to `startAnimation()`, given the `Animation` to apply to itself. This is the technique we will be seeing used in the examples in this chapter.

A Quirky Translation

Animation takes some getting used to. Frequently, it takes a fair bit of experimentation to get it all working as you wish. This is particularly true of `TranslateAnimation`, as not everything about it is intuitive, even to authors of Android books.

Mechanics of Translation

The simple constructor for `TranslateAnimation` takes four parameters describing how the widget should move: the before and after X offsets from the current position, and the before and after Y offsets from the current position. The Android documentation refers to these as `fromXDelta`, `toXDelta`, `fromYDelta`, and `toYDelta`.

In Android's pixel-space, an (X,Y) coordinate of (0,0) represents the upper-left corner of the screen. Hence, if `toXDelta` is greater than `fromXDelta`, the widget will move to the right, if `toYDelta` is greater than `fromYDelta`, the widget will move down, and so on.

Imagining a Sliding Panel

Some Android applications employ a sliding panel, one that is off-screen most of the time but can be called up by the user (e.g., via a menu) when desired. When anchored at the bottom of the screen, the effect is akin to the Android menu system, with a container that slides up from the bottom and slides down and out when being removed. However, while menus are limited to menu choices, Android's animation framework lets one create a sliding panel containing whatever widgets you might want.

One way to implement such a panel is to have a container (e.g., a LinearLayout) whose contents are absent (GONE) when the panel is closed and is present (VISIBLE) when the drawer is open. If we simply toggled setVisibility() using the aforementioned values, though, the panel would wink open and closed immediately, without any sort of animation. So, instead, we want to:

- Make the panel visible and animate it up from the bottom of the screen when we open the panel
- Animate it down to the bottom of the screen and make the panel gone when we close the panel

The Aftermath

This brings up a key point with respect to TranslateAnimation: the animation temporarily moves the widget, but if you want the widget to stay where it is when the animation is over, you have to handle that yourself. Otherwise, the widget will snap back to its original position when the animation completes.

In the case of the panel opening, we handle that via the transition from GONE to VISIBLE. Technically speaking, the panel is always "open", in that we are not, in the end, changing its position. But when the body of the panel is GONE, it takes up no space on the screen; when we make it VISIBLE, it takes up whatever space it is supposed to.

Animating Widgets

Later in this chapter, we will cover how to use animation listeners to accomplish this end for closing the panel.

Introducing SlidingPanel

With all that said, turn your attention to the Animation/SlidingPanel project and, in particular, the SlidingPanel class.

This class implements a layout that works as a panel, anchored to the bottom of the screen. A toggle() method can be called by the activity to hide or show the panel. The panel itself is a LinearLayout, so you can put whatever contents you want in there.

We use two flavors of TranslateAnimation, one for opening the panel and one for closing it.

Here is the opening animation:

```
anim=new TranslateAnimation(0.0f, 0.0f,
                            getLayoutParams().height,
                            0.0f);
```

Our fromXDelta and toXDelta are both 0, since we are not shifting the panel's position along the horizontal axis. Our fromYDelta is the panel's height according to its layout parameters (representing how big we want the panel to be), because we want the panel to start the animation at the bottom of the screen; our toYDelta is 0 because we want the panel to be at its "natural" open position at the end of the animation.

Conversely, here is the closing animation:

```
anim=new TranslateAnimation(0.0f, 0.0f, 0.0f,
                            getLayoutParams().height);
```

It has the same basic structure, except the Y values are reversed, since we want the panel to start open and animate to a closed position.

The result is a container that can be closed:

Figure 28. The SlidingPanel sample application, with the panel closed

...or open, in this case toggled via a menu choice in the SlidingPanelDemo activity:

Figure 29. The SlidingPanel sample application, with the panel open

Using the Animation

When setting up an animation, you also need to indicate how long the animation should take. This is done by calling setDuration() on the animation, providing the desired length of time in milliseconds.

When we are ready with the animation, we simply call startAnimation() on the SlidingPanel itself, causing it to move as specified by the TranslateAnimation instance.

Fading To Black. Or Some Other Color.

AlphaAnimation allows you to fade a widget in or out by making it less or more transparent. The greater the transparency, the more the widget appears to be "fading".

Alpha Numbers

You may be used to alpha channels, when used in #AARRGGBB color notation, or perhaps when working with alpha-capable image formats like PNG.

Similarly, `AlphaAnimation` allows you to change the alpha channel for an entire widget, from fully-solid to fully-transparent.

In Android, a float value of `1.0` indicates a fully-solid widget, while a value of `0.0` indicates a fully-transparent widget. Values in between, of course, represent various amounts of transparency.

Hence, it is common for an `AlphaAnimation` to either start at `1.0` and smoothly change the alpha to `0.0` (a fade) or vice versa.

Animations in XML

With `TranslateAnimation`, we showed how to construct the animation in Java source code. One can also create animation resources, which define the animations using XML. This is similar to the process for defining layouts, albeit much simpler.

For example, there is a second animation project, `Animation/SlidingPanelEx`, which demonstrates a panel that fades out as it is closed. In there, you will find a `res/anim/` directory, which is where animation resources should reside. In there, you will find `fade.xml`:

```
<?xml version="1.0" encoding="utf-8"?>
<alpha xmlns:android="http://schemas.android.com/apk/res/android"
  android:fromAlpha="1.0"
  android:toAlpha="0.0" />
```

The name of the root element indicates the type of animation (in this case, alpha for an `AlphaAnimation`). The attributes specify the characteristics of the animation, in this case a fade from `1.0` to `0.0` on the alpha channel.

This XML is the same as calling `new AlphaAnimation(1.0f,0.0f)` in Java.

Using XML Animations

To make use of XML-defined animations, you need to inflate them, much as you might inflate a `View` or `Menu` resource. This is accomplished by using the `loadAnimation()` static method on the `AnimationUtils` class:

```
fadeOut=AnimationUtils.loadAnimation(ctxt, R.anim.fade);
```

Here, we are loading our fade animation, given a `Context`. This is being put into an `Animation` variable, so we neither know nor care that this particular XML that we are loading defines an `AlphaAnimation` instead of, say, a `RotateAnimation`.

When It's All Said And Done

Sometimes, you need to take action when an animation completes.

For example, when we close the panel, we want to use a `TranslationAnimation` to slide it down from the open position to closed...then *keep* it closed. With the system used in `SlidingPanel`, keeping the panel closed is a matter of calling `setVisibility()` on the contents with `GONE`.

However, you cannot do that when the animation begins; otherwise, the panel is gone by the time you try to animate its motion.

Instead, you need to arrange to have it be gone when the animation ends. To do that, you use a animation listener.

An animation listener is simply an instance of the `AnimationListener` interface, provided to an animation via `setAnimationListener()`. The listener will be invoked when the starts, ends, or repeats (the latter courtesy of `CycleInterpolator`, discussed later in this chapter). You can put logic in the `onAnimationEnd()` callback in the listener to take action when the animation finishes.

Animating Widgets

For example, here is the `AnimationListener` for `SlidingPanel`:

```
Animation.AnimationListener collapseListener=new Animation.AnimationListener() {
  public void onAnimationEnd(Animation animation) {
    setVisibility(View.GONE);
  }

  public void onAnimationRepeat(Animation animation) {
    // not needed
  }

  public void onAnimationStart(Animation animation) {
    // not needed
  }
};
```

All we do is set the `ImageButton`'s image to be the upward-pointing arrow and setting our content's visibility to be `GONE`, thereby closing the panel.

Hit The Accelerator

In addition to the `Animation` classes themselves, Android also provides a set of `Interpolator` classes. These provide instructions for how an animation is supposed to behave during its operating period.

For example, the `AccelerateInterpolator` indicates that, during the duration of an animation, the rate of change of the animation should begin slowly and accelerate until the end. When applied to a `TranslateAnimation`, for example, the sliding movement will start out slowly and pick up speed until the movement is complete.

There are several implementations of the Interpolator interface besides `AccelerateInterpolator`, including:

- `AccelerateDecelerateInterpolator`, which starts slowly, picks up speed in the middle, and slows down again at the end
- `DecelerateInterpolator`, which starts quickly and slows down towards the end
- `LinearInterpolator`, the default, which indicates the animation should proceed smoothly from start to finish

- `CycleInterpolator`, which repeats an animation for a number of cycles, following the AccelerateDecelerateInterpolator pattern (slow, then fast, then slow)

To apply an interpolator to an animation, simply call `setInterpolator()` on the animation with the `Interpolator` instance, such as the following line from `SlidingPanel`:

```
anim.setInterpolator(new AccelerateInterpolator(1.0f));
```

You can also specify one of the stock interpolators via the `android:interpolator` attribute in your animation XML file.

Animate. Set. Match.

For the `Animation/SlidingPanelEx` project, though, we want the panel to slide open, but also fade when it slides closed. This implies two animations working at the same time (a fade and a slide). Android supports this via the `AnimationSet` class.

An `AnimationSet` is itself an `Animation` implementation. Following the composite design pattern, it simply cascades the major `Animation` events to each of the animations in the set.

To create a set, just create an `AnimationSet` instance, add the animations, and configure the set. For example, here is the logic from the `SlidingPanel` implementation in `Animation/SlidingPanelEx`:

```
public void toggle() {
  TranslateAnimation anim=null;
  AnimationSet set=new AnimationSet(true);

  isOpen=!isOpen;

  if (isOpen) {
    setVisibility(View.VISIBLE);
    anim=new TranslateAnimation(0.0f, 0.0f,
                                getLayoutParams().height,
                                0.0f);
  }
```

```
else {
    anim=new TranslateAnimation(0.0f, 0.0f, 0.0f,
                                getLayoutParams().height);
    anim.setAnimationListener(collapseListener);
    set.addAnimation(fadeOut);
}

set.addAnimation(anim);
set.setDuration(speed);
set.setInterpolator(new AccelerateInterpolator(1.0f));
startAnimation(set);
}
```

If the panel is to be opened, we make the contents visible (so we can animate the motion upwards), and create a TranslateAnimation for the upward movement. If the panel is to be closed, we create a TranslateAnimation for the downward movement, but also add a pre-defined AlphaAnimation (fadeOut) to an AnimationSet. In either case, we add the TranslateAnimation to the set, give the set a duration and interpolator, and run the animation.

CHAPTER 7

Playing Media

Pretty much every phone claiming to be a "smartphone" has the ability to at least play back music, if not video. Even many more ordinary phones are full-fledged MP3 players, in addition to offering ringtones and whatnot.

Not surprisingly, Android has multimedia support for you, as a developer, to build your own games, media players, and so on.

This chapter is focused on audio and video playback; other chapters will tackle media input, including the camera and audio recording.

Get Your Media On

In Android, you have five different places you can pull media clips from – one of these will hopefully fit your needs:

1. You can package media clips as raw resources (`res/raw` in your project), so they are bundled with your application. The benefit is that you're guaranteed the clips will be there; the downside is that they cannot be replaced without upgrading the application.

2. You can package media clips as assets (`assets/` in your project) and reference them via `file:///android_asset/` URLs in a `Uri`. The benefit over raw resources is that this location works with APIs that expect `Uri` parameters instead of resource IDs. The downside –

assets are only replaceable when the application is upgraded – remains.

3. You can store media in an application-local directory, such as content you download off the Internet. Your media may or may not be there, and your storage space isn't infinite, but you can replace the media as needed.

4. You can store media – or reference media that the user has stored herself – that is on an SD card. There is likely more storage space on the card than there is on the device, and you can replace the media as needed, but other applications have access to the SD card as well.

5. You can, in some cases, stream media off the Internet, bypassing any local storage, as with the StreamFurious[20] application

Internet streaming is tricky, particularly for video, and is well beyond the scope of this book. For the T-Mobile G1, the recommended approach for anything of significant size is to put it on the SD card, as there is very little on-board flash memory for file storage.

Making Noise

The crux of playing back audio comes in the form of the `MediaPlayer` class. With it, you can feed it an audio clip, start/stop/pause playback, and get notified on key events, such as when the clip is ready to be played or is done playing.

You have three ways to set up a `MediaPlayer` and tell it what audio clip to play:

1. If the clip is a raw resource, use `MediaPlayer.create()` and provide the resource ID of the clip

2. If you have a `Uri` to the clip, use the `Uri`-flavored version of `MediaPlayer.create()`

---

20 http://www.streamfurious.com/

Playing Media

3. If you have a string path to the clip, just create a `MediaPlayer` using the default constructor, then call `setDataSource()` with the path to the clip

Next, you need to call `prepare()` or `prepareAsync()`. Both will set up the clip to be ready to play, such as fetching the first few seconds off the file or stream. The `prepare()` method is synchronous; as soon as it returns, the clip is ready to play. The `prepareAsync()` method is asynchronous – more on how to use this version later.

Once the clip is prepared, `start()` begins playback, `pause()` pauses playback (with `start()` picking up playback where `pause()` paused), and `stop()` ends playback. One caveat: you cannot simply call `start()` again on the `MediaPlayer` once you have called `stop()` – we'll cover a workaround a bit later in this section.

To see this in action, take a look at the `Media/Audio` sample project. The layout is pretty trivial, with three buttons and labels for play, pause, and stop:

```xml
<?xml version="1.0" encoding="utf-8"?>
<LinearLayout xmlns:android="http://schemas.android.com/apk/res/android"
    android:orientation="vertical"
    android:layout_width="fill_parent"
    android:layout_height="fill_parent"
    >
  <LinearLayout
    android:orientation="horizontal"
    android:layout_width="fill_parent"
    android:layout_height="wrap_content"
    android:padding="4px"
  >
    <ImageButton android:id="@+id/play"
      android:src="@drawable/play"
      android:layout_height="wrap_content"
      android:layout_width="wrap_content"
      android:paddingRight="4px"
      android:enabled="false"
    />
    <TextView
      android:text="Play"
      android:layout_width="fill_parent"
      android:layout_height="fill_parent"
      android:gravity="center_vertical"
      android:layout_gravity="center_vertical"
```

```xml
      android:textAppearance="?android:attr/textAppearanceLarge"
      />
  </LinearLayout>
  <LinearLayout
    android:orientation="horizontal"
    android:layout_width="fill_parent"
    android:layout_height="wrap_content"
    android:padding="4px"
    >
    <ImageButton android:id="@+id/pause"
      android:src="@drawable/pause"
      android:layout_height="wrap_content"
      android:layout_width="wrap_content"
      android:paddingRight="4px"
      />
    <TextView
      android:text="Pause"
      android:layout_width="fill_parent"
      android:layout_height="fill_parent"
      android:gravity="center_vertical"
      android:layout_gravity="center_vertical"
      android:textAppearance="?android:attr/textAppearanceLarge"
      />
  </LinearLayout>
  <LinearLayout
    android:orientation="horizontal"
    android:layout_width="fill_parent"
    android:layout_height="wrap_content"
    android:padding="4px"
    >
    <ImageButton android:id="@+id/stop"
      android:src="@drawable/stop"
      android:layout_height="wrap_content"
      android:layout_width="wrap_content"
      android:paddingRight="4px"
      />
    <TextView
      android:text="Stop"
      android:layout_width="fill_parent"
      android:layout_height="fill_parent"
      android:gravity="center_vertical"
      android:layout_gravity="center_vertical"
      android:textAppearance="?android:attr/textAppearanceLarge"
      />
  </LinearLayout>
</LinearLayout>
```

The Java, of course, is where things get interesting:

```java
public class AudioDemo extends Activity
  implements MediaPlayer.OnCompletionListener {

  private ImageButton play;
```

```java
  private ImageButton pause;
  private ImageButton stop;
  private MediaPlayer mp;

  @Override
  public void onCreate(Bundle icicle) {
    super.onCreate(icicle);
    setContentView(R.layout.main);

    play=(ImageButton)findViewById(R.id.play);
    pause=(ImageButton)findViewById(R.id.pause);
    stop=(ImageButton)findViewById(R.id.stop);

    play.setOnClickListener(new View.OnClickListener() {
      public void onClick(View view) {
        play();
      }
    });

    pause.setOnClickListener(new View.OnClickListener() {
      public void onClick(View view) {
        pause();
      }
    });

    stop.setOnClickListener(new View.OnClickListener() {
      public void onClick(View view) {
        stop();
      }
    });

    setup();
  }

  @Override
  public void onDestroy() {
    super.onDestroy();

    if (stop.isEnabled()) {
      stop();
    }
  }

  public void onCompletion(MediaPlayer mp) {
    stop();
  }

  private void play() {
    mp.start();

    play.setEnabled(false);
    pause.setEnabled(true);
    stop.setEnabled(true);
  }
```

```java
private void stop() {
  mp.stop();
  mp.release();
  setup();
}

private void pause() {
  mp.pause();

  play.setEnabled(true);
  pause.setEnabled(false);
  stop.setEnabled(true);
}

private void loadClip() {
  try {
    mp=MediaPlayer.create(this, R.raw.clip);
    mp.setOnCompletionListener(this);
  }
  catch (Throwable t) {
    goBlooey(t);
  }
}

private void setup() {
  loadClip();
  play.setEnabled(true);
  pause.setEnabled(false);
  stop.setEnabled(false);
}

private void goBlooey(Throwable t) {
  AlertDialog.Builder builder=new AlertDialog.Builder(this);

  builder
    .setTitle("Exception!")
    .setMessage(t.toString())
    .setPositiveButton("OK", null)
    .show();
}
}
```

In onCreate(), we wire up the three buttons to appropriate callbacks, then call setup(). In setup(), we create our MediaPlayer, set to play a clip we package in the project as a raw resource. We also configure the activity itself as the completion listener, so we find out when the clip is over. Note that, since we use the static create() method on MediaPlayer, we have already implicitly called prepare(), so we do not need to call that separately ourselves.

Playing Media

The buttons simply work the MediaPlayer and toggle each others' states, via appropriately-named callbacks. So, play() starts MediaPlayer playback, pause() pauses playback, and stop() stops playback and resets our MediaPlayer to play again. The stop() callback is also used for when the audio clip completes of its own accord.

To reset the MediaPlayer, the stop() callback calls release() on the existing MediaPlayer (to release its resources), then calls setup() again, discarding the used MediaPlayer and starting a fresh one.

The UI is nothing special, but we are more interested in the audio in this sample, anyway:

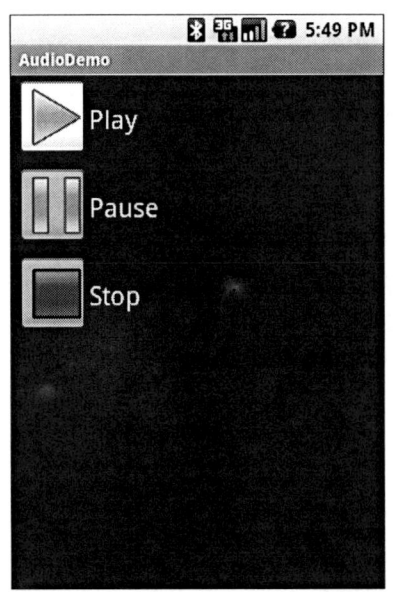

Figure 30. The AudioDemo sample application

Moving Pictures

Video clips get their own widget, the VideoView. Put it in a layout, feed it an MP4 video clip, and you get playback!

For example, take a look at this layout, from the Media/Video sample project:

103

```xml
<?xml version="1.0" encoding="utf-8"?>
<LinearLayout xmlns:android="http://schemas.android.com/apk/res/android"
    android:orientation="vertical"
    android:layout_width="fill_parent"
    android:layout_height="fill_parent"
    >
  <VideoView
    android:id="@+id/video"
      android:layout_width="fill_parent"
      android:layout_height="fill_parent"
    />
</LinearLayout>
```

The layout is simply a full-screen video player. Whether it will use the full screen will be dependent on the video clip, its aspect ratio, and whether you have the device (or emulator) in portrait or landscape mode.

Wiring up the Java is almost as simple:

```java
public class VideoDemo extends Activity {
  private VideoView video;
  private MediaController ctlr;

  @Override
  public void onCreate(Bundle icicle) {
    super.onCreate(icicle);
    getWindow().setFormat(PixelFormat.TRANSLUCENT);
    setContentView(R.layout.main);

    File clip=new File("/sdcard/test.mp4");

    if (clip.exists()) {
      video=(VideoView)findViewById(R.id.video);
      video.setVideoPath(clip.getAbsolutePath());

      ctlr=new MediaController(this);
      ctlr.setMediaPlayer(video);
      video.setMediaController(ctlr);
      video.requestFocus();
    }
  }
}
```

The biggest trick with VideoView is getting a video clip onto the device. While VideoView does support some streaming video, the requirements on the MP4 file are fairly stringent. If you want to be able to play a wider array of video clips, you need to have them on the device, preferably on an SD card.

Playing Media

The crude VideoDemo class assumes there is an MP4 file in /sdcard/test.mp4 on your emulator. To make this a reality:

1. Find a clip, such as Aaron Rosenberg's *Documentaries and You* from Duke University's Center for the Study of the Public Domain's Moving Image Contest[21], which was used in the creation of this book

2. Use mksdcard (in the Android SDK's tools directory) to create a suitably-sized SD card image (e.g., mksdcard 128M sd.img)

3. Use the -sdcard switch when launching the emulator, providing the path to your SD card image, so the SD card is "mounted" when the emulator starts

4. Use the adb push command (or DDMS or the equivalent in your IDE) to copy the MP4 file into /sdcard/test.mp4

Once there, the Java code shown above will give you a working video player:

Figure 31. The VideoDemo sample application, showing a Creative Commons-licensed video clip

Tapping on the video will pop up the playback controls:

---
21 http://www.law.duke.edu/cspd/contest/finalists/

Figure 32. The VideoDemo sample application, with the media controls displayed

The video will scale based on space, as shown in this rotated view of the emulator (<Ctrl>-<F12>):

Figure 33. The VideoDemo sample application, in landscape mode, with the video clip scaled to fit

Note that playback may be rather jerky in the emulator, depending on the power of the PC that is hosting the emulator. For example, on a Pentium-M

1.6GHz PC, playback in the emulator is extremely jerky, while playback on the T-Mobile G1 is very smooth.

CHAPTER 8

Using the Camera

Most Android devices will have a camera, since they are fairly commonplace on mobile devices these days. You, as an Android developer, can take advantage of the camera, for everything from snapping tourist photos to scanning barcodes. For simple operations, the APIs needed to use the camera are fairly straight-forward, requiring a bit of boilerplate code plus your own unique application logic.

What is a problem is using the camera with the emulator. The emulator does not emulate a camera, nor is there a convenient way to pretend there are pictures via DDMS or similar tools. For the purposes of this chapter, it is assumed you have access to an actual Android-powered hardware device and can use it for development purposes.

Sneaking a Peek

First, it is fairly common for a camera-using application to support a preview mode, to show the user what the camera sees. This will help make sure the camera is lined up on the subject properly, whether there is sufficient lighting, etc.

So, let us take a look at how to create an application that shows such a live preview. The code snippets shown in this section are pulled from the Camera/Preview sample project.

The Permission

First, you need permission to use the camera. That way, when end users install your application off of the Internet, they will be notified that you intend to use the camera, so they can determine if they deem that appropriate for your application.

You simply need the CAMERA permission in your AndroidManifest.xml file, along with whatever other permissions your application logic might require. Here is the manifest from the Camera/Preview sample project:

```xml
<?xml version="1.0" encoding="utf-8"?>
<manifest xmlns:android="http://schemas.android.com/apk/res/android"
    package="com.commonsware.android.camera"
    android:versionCode="1"
    android:versionName="1.0">
  <uses-permission android:name="android.permission.CAMERA" />
  <application android:label="@string/app_name">
    <activity android:name=".PreviewDemo"
              android:label="@string/app_name"
              android:configChanges="keyboardHidden|orientation"
              android:screenOrientation="landscape"
              android:theme="@android:style/Theme.NoTitleBar.Fullscreen">
      <intent-filter>
        <action android:name="android.intent.action.MAIN" />
        <category android:name="android.intent.category.LAUNCHER" />
      </intent-filter>
    </activity>
  </application>
</manifest>
```

Also note a few other things about our PreviewDemo activity as registered in this manifest:

- We use android:configChanges = "keyboardHidden|orientation" to ensure we control what happens when the keyboard is hidden or exposed, rather than have Android rotate the screen for us
- We use android:screenOrientation = "landscape" to tell Android we are always in landscape mode. This is necessary because of a bit of a bug in the camera preview logic, such that it works best in landscape mode.

Using the Camera

- We use android:theme = "@android:style/Fullscreen" to get rid of the title bar and status bar, so the preview is truly full-screen (e.g., 480x320 on a T-Mobile G1).

The SurfaceView

Next, you need a layout supporting a SurfaceView. SurfaceView is used as a raw canvas for displaying all sorts of graphics outside of the realm of your ordinary widgets. In this case, Android knows how to display a live look at what the camera sees on a SurfaceView, to serve as a preview pane.

For example, here is a full-screen SurfaceView layout as used by the PreviewDemo activity:

```xml
<?xml version="1.0" encoding="utf-8"?>
<android.view.SurfaceView
xmlns:android="http://schemas.android.com/apk/res/android"
    android:id="@+id/preview"
    android:layout_width="fill_parent"
    android:layout_height="fill_parent"
    >
</android.view.SurfaceView>
```

The Camera

The biggest step, of course, is telling Android to use the camera service and tie a camera to the SurfaceView to show the actual preview. We will also eventually need the camera service to take real pictures, as will be described in the next section.

There are three major components to getting picture preview working:

1. The SurfaceView, as defined in our layout
2. A SurfaceHolder, which is a means of controlling behavior of the SurfaceView, such as its size, or being notified when the surface changes, such as when the preview is started
3. A Camera, obtained from the open() static method on the Camera class

Using the Camera

To wire these together, we first need to:

- Get the `SurfaceHolder` for our `SurfaceView` via `getHolder()`
- Register a `SurfaceHolder.Callback` with the `SurfaceHolder`, so we are notified when the `SurfaceView` is ready or changes
- Tell the `SurfaceView` (via the `SurfaceHolder`) that it has the `SURFACE_TYPE_PUSH_BUFFERS` type (`setType()`) – this indicates something in the system will be updating the `SurfaceView` and providing the bitmap data to display

This gives us a configured `SurfaceView` (shown below), but we still need to tie in the `Camera`.

```
@Override
public void onCreate(Bundle savedInstanceState) {
  super.onCreate(savedInstanceState);
  setContentView(R.layout.main);

  preview=(SurfaceView)findViewById(R.id.preview);
  previewHolder=preview.getHolder();
  previewHolder.addCallback(surfaceCallback);
  previewHolder.setType(SurfaceHolder.SURFACE_TYPE_PUSH_BUFFERS);
}
```

A `Camera` object has a `setPreviewDisplay()` method that takes a `SurfaceHolder` and, as you might expect, arranges for the camera preview to be displayed on the associated `SurfaceView`. However, the `SurfaceView` may not be ready immediately after being changed into `SURFACE_TYPE_PUSH_BUFFERS` mode. So, while the previous setup work could be done in `onCreate()`, you should wait until the `SurfaceHolder.Callback` has its `surfaceCreated()` method called, then register the `Camera`:

```
public void surfaceCreated(SurfaceHolder holder) {
  camera=Camera.open();

  try {
    camera.setPreviewDisplay(previewHolder);
  }
  catch (Throwable t) {
    Log.e("PreviewDemo-surfaceCallback",
          "Exception in setPreviewDisplay()", t);
    Toast
      .makeText(PreviewDemo.this, t.getMessage(), Toast.LENGTH_LONG)
      .show();
```

```
    }
}
```

Next, once the SurfaceView is set up and sized by Android, we need to pass configuration data to the Camera, so it knows how big to draw the preview. Since the preview pane is not a fixed size – it might vary based on hardware – we cannot safely pre-determine the size. It is simplest to wait for our SurfaceHolder.Callback to have its surfaceChanged() method called, when we are told the size of the surface. Then, we can pour that information into a Camera.Parameters object, update the Camera with those parameters, and have the Camera show the preview images via startPreview():

```
public void surfaceChanged(SurfaceHolder holder,
                    int format, int width,
                    int height) {
  Camera.Parameters parameters=camera.getParameters();

  parameters.setPreviewSize(width, height);
  camera.setParameters(parameters);
  camera.startPreview();
}
```

Eventually, the preview needs to stop. In this particular case, that will be as the activity is being destroyed. It is important to release the Camera at this time – for many devices, there is only one physical camera, so only one activity can be using it at a time. Our SurfaceHolder.Callback will be told, via surfaceDestroyed(), when it is being closed up, and we can stop the preview (stopPreview()), release the camera (release()), and let go of it (camera = null) at that point:

```
public void surfaceDestroyed(SurfaceHolder holder) {
  camera.stopPreview();
  camera.release();
  camera=null;
}
```

If you compile and run the Camera/Preview sample application, you will see, on-screen, what the camera sees.

Here is the full SurfaceHolder.Callback implementation:

```java
SurfaceHolder.Callback surfaceCallback=new SurfaceHolder.Callback() {
  public void surfaceCreated(SurfaceHolder holder) {
    camera=Camera.open();

    try {
      camera.setPreviewDisplay(previewHolder);
    }
    catch (Throwable t) {
      Log.e("PreviewDemo-surfaceCallback",
          "Exception in setPreviewDisplay()", t);
      Toast
        .makeText(PreviewDemo.this, t.getMessage(), Toast.LENGTH_LONG)
        .show();
    }
  }

  public void surfaceChanged(SurfaceHolder holder,
                             int format, int width,
                             int height) {
    Camera.Parameters parameters=camera.getParameters();

    parameters.setPreviewSize(width, height);
    camera.setParameters(parameters);
    camera.startPreview();
  }

  public void surfaceDestroyed(SurfaceHolder holder) {
    camera.stopPreview();
    camera.release();
    camera=null;
  }
};
```

Image Is Everything

Showing the preview imagery is nice and all, but it is probably more important to actually take a picture now and again. The previews show the user what the camera sees, but we still need to let our application know what the camera sees at particular points in time.

In principle, this is easy. Where things get a bit complicated comes with ensuring the application (and device as a whole) has decent performance, not slowing down to process the pictures.

The code snippets shown in this section are pulled from the Camera/Picture sample project, which builds upon the Camera/Preview sample shown in the previous section.

Asking for a Format

We need to tell the Camera what sort of picture to take when we decide to take a picture. The two options are raw and JPEG.

At least, that is the theory.

In practice, the T-Mobile G1 does not support raw output, only JPEG. So, we need to tell the Camera that we want JPEG output.

That is merely a matter of calling setPictureFormat() on the Camera.Parameters object when we configure our Camera, using the value JPEG to indicate that we, indeed, want JPEG:

```java
public void surfaceChanged(SurfaceHolder holder,
                           int format, int width,
                           int height) {
  Camera.Parameters parameters=camera.getParameters();

  parameters.setPreviewSize(width, height);
  parameters.setPictureFormat(PixelFormat.JPEG);
  camera.setParameters(parameters);
  camera.startPreview();
}
```

Connecting the Camera Button

Somehow, your application will need to indicate when a picture should be taken. That could be via widgets on the UI, though in our samples here, the preview is full-screen.

An alternative is to use the camera hardware button. Like every hardware button other than the Home button, we can find out when the camera button is clicked via onKeyDown():

```
@Override
public boolean onKeyDown(int keyCode, KeyEvent event) {
  if (keyCode==KeyEvent.KEYCODE_CAMERA ||
      keyCode==KeyEvent.KEYCODE_SEARCH) {
    takePicture();

    return(true);
  }

  return(super.onKeyDown(keyCode, event));
}
```

Since the HTC Magic does not have a hardware camera button, we also watch for KEYCODE_SEARCH for the dedicated search key, which is in the upper-right portion of the Magic's face when the device is held in landscape mode.

Taking a Picture

Once it is time to take a picture, all you need to do is:

- Stop the preview
- Tell the Camera to takePicture()

The takePicture() method takes three parameters, all callback-style objects:

1. A "shutter" callback (Camera.ShutterCallback), which is notified when the picture has been captured by the hardware but the data is not yet available – you might use this to play a "camera click" sound
2. Callbacks to receive the image data, either in raw format or JPEG format

Since the T-Mobile G1 only supports JPEG output, and because we do not want to fuss with a shutter click, PictureDemo only passes in the third parameter to takePicture():

```
private void takePicture() {
  camera.stopPreview();
  camera.takePicture(null, null, photoCallback);
}
```

Using the Camera

The `Camera.PictureCallback` (`photoCallback`) needs to implement `onPictureTaken()`, which provides the picture data as a `byte[]`, plus the `Camera` object that took the picture. At this point, it is safe to start up the preview again.

Plus, of course, it would be nice to do something with that byte array.

The catch is that the byte array is going to be large – the T-Mobile G1 has a 3-megapixel camera, and future hardware is more likely to have richer hardware than that. Writing that to flash, or sending it over the network, or doing just about anything with the data, will be slow. Slow is fine...so long as it is not on the UI thread.

That means we need to do a little more work.

Using AsyncTask

In theory, we could just fork a background thread to save off the image data or do whatever it is we wanted done with it. However, we could wind up with several such threads, particularly if we are sending the image over the Internet and do not have a fast connection to our destination server.

Android 1.5 offers a work queue model, in the form of `AsyncTask`. `AsyncTask` manages a thread pool and work queue – all we need to do is hand it the work to be done.

So, we can create an `AsyncTask` implementation, called `SavePhotoTask`, as follows:

```
class SavePhotoTask extends AsyncTask<byte[], String, String> {
  @Override
  protected String doInBackground(byte[]... jpeg) {
    File photo=new File(Environment.getExternalStorageDirectory(),
                        "photo.jpg");

    if (photo.exists()) {
      photo.delete();
    }
```

Using the Camera

```
try {
  FileOutputStream fos=new FileOutputStream(photo.getPath());

  fos.write(jpeg[0]);
  fos.close();
}
catch (java.io.IOException e) {
  Log.e("PictureDemo", "Exception in photoCallback", e);
}

return(null);
}
}
```

Our `doInBackground()` implementation gets the byte array we received from Android. The byte array is simply the JPEG itself, so the data could be written to a file, transformed, sent to a Web service, converted into a `BitmapDrawable` for display on the screen or whatever.

In the case of `PictureDemo`, we take the simple approach of writing the JPEG file as `photo.jpg` in the root of the SD card. The byte array itself will be garbage collected once we are done saving it, so there is no explicit "free" operation we need to do to release that memory.

Finally, we arrange for our `PhotoCallback` to execute our `SavePhotoTask`:

```
Camera.PictureCallback photoCallback=new Camera.PictureCallback() {
  public void onPictureTaken(byte[] data, Camera camera) {
    new SavePhotoTask().execute(data);
    camera.startPreview();
  }
};
```

PART III – Advanced System

CHAPTER 9

Sensors

"Sensors" is Android's overall term for ways that Android can detect elements of the physical world around it, from magnetic flux to the movement of the device. Not all devices will have all possible sensors, and other sensors are likely to be added over time. In this chapter, we will explore what sensors are theoretically available and how to use a few of them that work on early Android devices like the T-Mobile G1.

The samples in this chapter assume that you have access to a piece of sensor-equipped Android hardware, such as a T-Mobile G1. The OpenIntents.org project has a sensor simulator[22] which you can also use, though the use of this tool is not covered here.

The author would like to thank Sean Catlin for code samples that helped clear up confusion surrounding the use of sensors.

The Sixth Sense. Or Possibly the Seventh.

In theory, Android supports the following sensor types:

- An accelerometer, that tells you the motion of the device in space through all three dimensions

- An ambient light sensor, telling you how bright or dark the surroundings are

---

22 http://www.openintents.org/en/node/23

- A magnetic field sensor, to tell you where magnetic north is (unless some other magnetic field is nearby, such as from an electrical motor)

- An orientation sensor, to tell you how the device is positioned in all three dimensions

- A proximity sensor, to tell you how far the device is from some other specific object

- A temperature sensor, to tell you the temperature of the surrounding environment

- A tricorder sensor, to turn the device into "a fully functional Tricorder"

Clearly, not all of these possible sensors are available today, such as the last one. What definitely are available today on the T-Mobile G1 are the accelerometer, the magnetic field sensor, and the orientation sensor.

To access any of these sensors, you need a SensorManager, found in the android.hardware package. Like other aspects of Android, the SensorManager is a system service, and as such is obtained via the getSystemService() method on your Activity or other Context:

```
mgr=(SensorManager)getSystemService(Context.SENSOR_SERVICE);
```

Orienting Yourself

In principle, to find out which direction is north, you would use the magnetic flux sensor and go through a lovely set of calculations to figure out the appropriate direction.

Fortunately for us, Android did all that as part of the orientation sensor...so long as the device is held flat in the horizontal plane (e.g., on a level tabletop).

Akin to the location services, there is no way to ask the SensorManager what the current value of a sensor is. Instead, you need to hook up a

SensorEventListener and respond to changes in the sensor values. To do this, simply call registerListener() with your SensorEventListener and the Sensor you wish to hear from. You can get the Sensor by asking the SensorManager for the default Sensor for a particular type. For example, from the Sensor/Compass sample project, here is where we register our listener:

```
mgr.registerListener(listener,
                mgr.getDefaultSensor(Sensor.TYPE_ORIENTATION),
                SensorManager.SENSOR_DELAY_UI);
```

Note that you also specify the rate at which sensor updates will be received. Here, we use SENSOR_DELAY_UI, but you could say SENSOR_DELAY_FASTEST or various other values.

It is important to unregister the listener when the activity closes down; otherwise, the application will never really terminate and the listener will get updates indefinitely. To do this, just call unregisterListener() from a likely location, such as onDestroy():

```
@Override
public void onDestroy() {
  super.onDestroy();
  mgr.unregisterListener(listener);
}
```

Your SensorEventListener implementation will need two methods. The one you probably will not use that often is onAccuracyChanged(), when you will be notified as a given sensor's accuracy changes from SENSOR_STATUS_ACCURACY_HIGH to SENSOR_STATUS_ACCURACY_MEDIUM to SENSOR_STATUS_ACCURACY_LOW to SENSOR_STATUS_UNRELIABLE.

The one you will use more commonly is onSensorChanged(), where you are provided a SensorEvent containing a float[] of values for the sensor. The tricky part is determining what these sensor values mean.

In the case of TYPE_ORIENTATION, the first of the supplied values represents the orientation of the device in degrees off of magnetic north. 90 degrees means east, 180 means south, and 270 means west, just like on a regular compass.

Sensors

In `Sensor/Compass`, we update a `TextView` with the each reading:

```
private SensorEventListener listener=new SensorEventListener() {
  public void onSensorChanged(SensorEvent e) {
    if (e.sensor.getType()==Sensor.TYPE_ORIENTATION) {
      degrees.setText(String.valueOf(e.values[0]));
    }
  }

  public void onAccuracyChanged(Sensor sensor, int accuracy) {
    // unused
  }
};
```

What you get is a trivial application showing where the top of the phone is pointing. Note that the sensor seems to take a bit to get initially stabilized, then will tend to lag actual motion a bit.

Figure 34. The CompassDemo application, showing a T-Mobile G1 pointing south-by-southeast

Steering Your Phone

In television commercials for other mobile devices, you may see them being used like a steering wheel, often times for playing a driving simulation game.

Android can do this too. You can see it in the Sensor/Steering sample application.

In the preceding section, we noted that TYPE_ORIENTATION returns in the first value of the float[] the orientation of the phone, compared to magnetic north, if the device is horizontal. When the device is held like a steering wheel, the second value of the float[] will change as the device is "steered".

This sample application is very similar to the Sensor/Compass one shown in the previous section. The biggest change comes in the SensorEventListener implementation:

```java
private SensorEventListener listener=new SensorEventListener() {
  public void onSensorChanged(SensorEvent e) {
    if (e.sensor.getType()==Sensor.TYPE_ORIENTATION) {
      float orientation=e.values[1];

      if (prevOrientation!=orientation) {
        if (prevOrientation<orientation) {
          steerLeft(orientation,
                  orientation-prevOrientation);
        }
        else {
          steerRight(orientation,
                  prevOrientation-orientation);
        }

        prevOrientation=e.values[1];
      }
    }
  }

  public void onAccuracyChanged(Sensor sensor, int accuracy) {
    // unused
  }
};
```

Sensors

Here, we track the previous orientation (prevOrientation) and call a steerLeft() or steerRight() method based on which direction the "wheel" is turned. For each, we provide the new current position of the wheel and the amount the wheel turned, measured in degrees.

The steerLeft() and steerRight() methods, in turn, simply dump their results to a "transcript": a TextView inside a ScrollView, set up to automatically keep scrolling to the bottom:

```
private void steerLeft(float position, float delta) {
  StringBuffer line=new StringBuffer("Steered left by ");

  line.append(String.valueOf(delta));
  line.append(" to ");
  line.append(String.valueOf(position));
  line.append("\n");
  transcript.setText(transcript.getText().toString()+line.toString());
  scroll.fullScroll(View.FOCUS_DOWN);
}

private void steerRight(float position, float delta) {
  StringBuffer line=new StringBuffer("Steered right by ");

  line.append(String.valueOf(delta));
  line.append(" to ");
  line.append(String.valueOf(position));
  line.append("\n");
  transcript.setText(transcript.getText().toString()+line.toString());
  scroll.fullScroll(View.FOCUS_DOWN);
}
```

The result is a log of the steering "events" as the device is turned like a steering wheel. Obviously, a real game would translate these events into game actions, such as changing your perspective of the driving course.

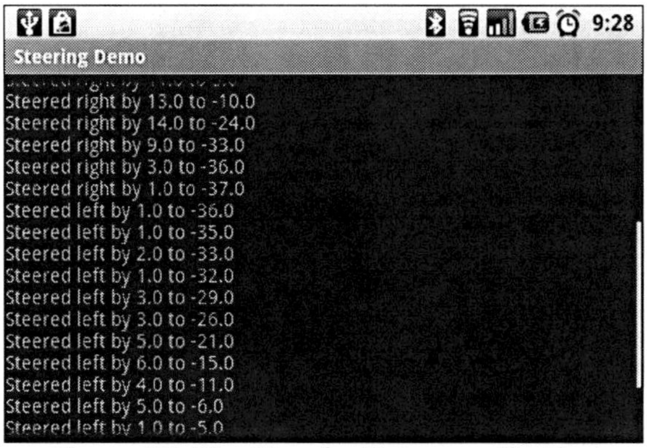

Sensors

Figure 35. The SteeringDemo application

Do "The Shake"

Another demo you often see with certain other mobile devices is shaking the device to cause some on-screen effect, such as rolling dice or scrambling puzzle pieces.

Android can do this as well, as you can see in the Sensor/Shaker sample application, with our data provided by the accelerometer sensor (TYPE_ACCELEROMETER).

What the accelerometer sensor provides is the accleration in each of three dimensions. At rest, the acceleration is equal to Earth's gravity (or the gravity of wherever you are, if you are not on Earth). When shaken, the acceleration should be higher than Earth's gravity – how much higher is dependent on how hard the device is being shaken. While the individual axes of acceleration might tell you, at any point in time, what direction the device is being shaken in, since a shaking action involves frequent constant changes in direction, what we really want to know is how fast the device is moving overall – a slow steady movement is not a shake, but something more aggressive is.

Once again, our UI output is simply a "transcript" TextView as before. This time, though, we separate out the actual shake-detection logic into a Shaker class which our ShakerDemo activity references, as shown below:

Sensors

```java
package com.commonsware.android.sensor;

import android.app.Activity;
import android.os.Bundle;
import android.util.Log;
import android.view.View;
import android.widget.ScrollView;
import android.widget.TextView;

public class ShakerDemo extends Activity
  implements Shaker.Callback {
  private Shaker shaker=null;
  private TextView transcript=null;
  private ScrollView scroll=null;

  @Override
  public void onCreate(Bundle savedInstanceState) {
    super.onCreate(savedInstanceState);
    setContentView(R.layout.main);

    transcript=(TextView)findViewById(R.id.transcript);
    scroll=(ScrollView)findViewById(R.id.scroll);

    shaker=new Shaker(this, 1.25d, 500, this);
  }

  @Override
  public void onDestroy() {
    super.onDestroy();

    shaker.close();
  }

  public void shakingStarted() {
    Log.d("ShakerDemo", "Shaking started!");
    transcript.setText(transcript.getText().toString()+"Shaking started\n");
    scroll.fullScroll(View.FOCUS_DOWN);
  }

  public void shakingStopped() {
    Log.d("ShakerDemo", "Shaking stopped!");
    transcript.setText(transcript.getText().toString()+"Shaking stopped\n");
    scroll.fullScroll(View.FOCUS_DOWN);
  }
}
```

The Shaker takes four parameters:

- A Context, so we can get access to the SensorManager service
- An indication of how hard a shake should qualify as a shake, expressed as a ratio applied to Earth's gravity, so a value of 1.25

Sensors

means the shake has to be 25% stronger than gravity to be considered a shake

- An amount of time with below-threshold acceleration, after which the shake is considered "done"
- A `Shaker.Callback` object that will be notified when a shake starts and stops

While in this case, the callback methods (implemented on the `ShakerDemo` activity itself) simply log shake events to the transcript, a "real" application would, say, start an animation of dice rolling when the shake starts and end the animation shortly after the shake ends.

The `Shaker` simply converts the three individual acceleration components into a combined acceleration value (square root of the sum of the squares), then compares that value to Earth's gravity. If the ratio is higher than the supplied threshold, then we consider the device to be presently shaking, and we call the `shakingStarted()` callback method if the device was not shaking before. Once shaking ends, and time elapses, we call `shakingStopped()` on the callback object and assume that the shake has ended. A more robust implementation of `Shaker` would take into account the possibility that the sensor will not be updated for a while after the shake ends, though in reality, normal human movement will ensure that there are some sensor updates, so we can find out when the shaking ends.

```java
package com.commonsware.android.sensor;

import android.content.Context;
import android.hardware.Sensor;
import android.hardware.SensorEvent;
import android.hardware.SensorEventListener;
import android.hardware.SensorManager;
import android.os.SystemClock;
import java.util.ArrayList;
import java.util.List;

public class Shaker {
  private SensorManager mgr=null;
  private long lastShakeTimestamp=0;
  private double threshold=1.0d;
  private long gap=0;
  private Shaker.Callback cb=null;
```

```java
public Shaker(Context ctxt, double threshold, long gap,
              Shaker.Callback cb) {
  this.threshold=threshold*threshold;
  this.threshold=this.threshold
                 *SensorManager.GRAVITY_EARTH
                 *SensorManager.GRAVITY_EARTH;
  this.gap=gap;
  this.cb=cb;

  mgr=(SensorManager)ctxt.getSystemService(Context.SENSOR_SERVICE);
  mgr.registerListener(listener,
                       mgr.getDefaultSensor(Sensor.TYPE_ACCELEROMETER),
                       SensorManager.SENSOR_DELAY_UI);
}

public void close() {
  mgr.unregisterListener(listener);
}

private void isShaking() {
  long now=SystemClock.uptimeMillis();

  if (lastShakeTimestamp==0) {
    lastShakeTimestamp=now;

    if (cb!=null) {
      cb.shakingStarted();
    }
  }
  else {
    lastShakeTimestamp=now;
  }
}

private void isNotShaking() {
  long now=SystemClock.uptimeMillis();

  if (lastShakeTimestamp>0) {
    if (now-lastShakeTimestamp>gap) {
      lastShakeTimestamp=0;

      if (cb!=null) {
        cb.shakingStopped();
      }
    }
  }
}

public interface Callback {
  void shakingStarted();
  void shakingStopped();
}

private SensorEventListener listener=new SensorEventListener() {
  public void onSensorChanged(SensorEvent e) {
```

```java
    if (e.sensor.getType()==Sensor.TYPE_ACCELEROMETER) {
      double netForce=e.values[0]*e.values[0];

      netForce+=e.values[1]*e.values[1];
      netForce+=e.values[2]*e.values[2];

      if (threshold<netForce) {
        isShaking();
      }
      else {
        isNotShaking();
      }
    }
  }

  public void onAccuracyChanged(Sensor sensor, int accuracy) {
    // unused
  }
};
}
```

All the transcript shows, of course, is when shaking starts and stops:

Figure 36. The ShakerDemo application, showing a pair of shakes

CHAPTER 10

Databases and Content Providers

In the abstract, working with SQLite databases and Android-style content providers is fairly straight-forward. Each supports a CRUD-style interface (`query()`, `insert()`, `update()`, `delete()`) using `Cursor` objects for query results. While implementing a `ContentProvider` is no picnic for non-SQLite data stores, everything else is fairly rote.

In reality, though, databases and content providers cause more than their fair share of hassles. Mostly, this comes from everything *outside* of simple CRUD operations, such as:

- How do we get a database into our application?
- How do we get data into our application on initial install? On an update?
- Where is the documentation for the built-in Android content providers?
- How do we deal with joins between data stores, such as merging contacts with our own database data?

In this chapter, we explore these issues, to show how you can better work with databases and content providers in the real world.

Distributed Data

Some databases used by Android applications naturally start empty. For example, a "password safe" probably has no passwords when initially launched by the user, and an expense-tracking application probably does not have any expenses recorded at the outset.

However, sometimes, there are databases that need to ship with an application that must be pre-populated with data. For example, you might be implementing an online catalog, with a database of items for sale installed with the application and updated as needed via calls to some Web service. The same structure would hold true for any sort of reference, from chemicals to word translations to historical sports records.

Unfortunately, there is no way to ship a database with data in it via the Android APK packaging mechanism. An APK is an executable blob, from the standpoint of Android and Dalvik. More importantly, it is stored read-only in a ZIP file, which makes updates to that data doubly impossible.

The next-best option is to ship your data with the application by some other means and load it into a newly-created database when the application is first run. This does involve two copies of the data: the original in your application and the working copy in the database. That may seem wasteful in terms of space. However, courtesy of ZIP compression, the original copy may not take up all that much space. Also, you can turn this into a feature, offering some sort of "reset" mechanism to reload the working database from the original if needed.

The challenge then becomes how to package the database contents into the APK and load it into the working database. Ideally, this involves as little work as possible from the developer, can fit into the existing build system, and can take advantage of existing database manipulation tools (versus, say, hand-writing hundreds of SQL INSERT statements).

Databases and Content Providers

Note that another possibility exists: package the binary SQLite database file[23] in the APK (e.g., in res/raw/) and copy it into position using binary streams. This assumes the SQLite database file your development environment would create is the same as what is expected by the SQLite engine baked into Android. This can work, but is likely to be more prone to versioning issues – for example, if your development environment is upgraded to a newer SQLite that has a slightly different file format.

SQLite: On-Device, On-Desktop

This becomes much simpler when you realize that Android uses SQLite for the database, and SQLite works on just about every platform you might need. It is trivial to work with SQLite databases on your development workstation, even easier than working with databases inside an Android emulator or device.

The plan, therefore, is to allow developers to create the database to be "shipped" as a SQLite database, then build tools that package the SQLite contents into the Android APK and turn it back into a database when the application needs it.

This allows developers to use whatever tools they want to manipulate the SQLite database, ranging from typical database management UIs to specialized conversion scripts to whatever.

To make this plan work, though, we need two bits of code:

1. We need something that extracts the data out of the SQLite database the developer has prepared and puts it someplace inside the Android APK

2. We need something that ties in with SQLiteOpenHelper that takes the APK-packaged data and turns it into an on-device database when the database is first accessed.

---

23 http://www.reigndesign.com/blog/using-your-own-sqlite-database-in-android-applications/

Exporting a Database

Fortunately, the `sqlite3` command-line executable that comes standard with SQLite offers a `.dump` command to dump the contents of a table as a series of SQL statements: one to create the table, plus the necessary SQL INSERT statements to populate it. All we need to do is tie this into the build system, so the act of compiling the APK also deals with the database.

You can find some sample code that handles this in the `Database/Packager` sample application. Specifically:

- There is a SQLite database containing data in the `db/` project directory – in this case, it is the database from the `ContentProvider/Constants` project from *The Busy Coder's Guide to Android Development*
- There is a `package_db.rb` Ruby script that wraps around the `.dump` command to export the data
- There is a change to the `build.xml` Ant script to use this Ruby script

The Ruby Script

You may or may not be a fan of Ruby. While this sample code shows this utility as a Ruby script, rest assured that SQLite has interfaces to most programming languages (though its Java support is not the strongest), so you can create your own edition of this script in whatever language suits you.

The script is fairly short:

```ruby
require 'rubygems'
require 'sqlite3'

Dir['db/*'].each do |path|
  db=SQLite3::Database.new(path)

  begin
    db.execute("SELECT name FROM sqlite_master WHERE type='table'") do |row|
      if ARGV.include?(row[0])
        puts `sqlite3 #{path} ".dump #{row[0]}"`
```

```
        end
      end
    ensure
      db.close
    end
end
```

It iterates over every file in the db/ directory and opens each as a SQLite database. It then queries the database for the list of tables (SELECT name FROM sqlite_master WHERE type = 'table'). Any table matching a table name passed in on the command line is assumed to be one needing to be exported, so it prints to stdout the results of the sqlite3 .dump command, run on that database and table. We use sqlite3 because there does not appear to be an API call that implements the .dump functionality.

To run this script, you need SQLite3 installed, with sqlite3 in your PATH, and you need the Ruby interpreter. You also need to run it from the project directory, with a db/ directory containing one or more database files.

Running the Ruby script will dump the specified tables as a set of SQL statements:

```
BEGIN TRANSACTION;
CREATE TABLE constants (_id INTEGER PRIMARY KEY AUTOINCREMENT, title TEXT, value REAL);
INSERT INTO "constants" VALUES(1,'Gravity, Death Star I',3.53036142541896e-07);
INSERT INTO "constants" VALUES(2,'Gravity, Earth',9.80665016174316);
INSERT INTO "constants" VALUES(3,'Gravity, Jupiter',23.1200008392334);
INSERT INTO "constants" VALUES(4,'Gravity, Mars',3.71000003814697);
INSERT INTO "constants" VALUES(5,'Gravity, Mercury',3.70000004768372);
INSERT INTO "constants" VALUES(6,'Gravity, Moon',1.60000002384186);
INSERT INTO "constants" VALUES(7,'Gravity, Neptune',11.0);
INSERT INTO "constants" VALUES(8,'Gravity, Pluto',0.600000023841858);
INSERT INTO "constants" VALUES(9,'Gravity, Saturn',8.96000003814697);
INSERT INTO "constants" VALUES(10,'Gravity, Sun',275.0);
INSERT INTO "constants" VALUES(11,'Gravity, The Island',4.81516218185425);
INSERT INTO "constants" VALUES(12,'Gravity, Uranus',8.6899995803833);
INSERT INTO "constants" VALUES(13,'Gravity, Venus',8.86999988555908);
COMMIT;
```

In this case, the constants table is empty, so there are no SQL INSERT statements. However, you could easily add some rows to the constants table – perhaps constants not available in Android itself – and ship those along with the table schema.

Loading the Exported Database

The other end of his process is to take the raw SQL stores in res/raw/packaged_db.txt and "inflate" it at runtime into a database. Since SQLiteOpenHelper is designed to handle such operations, it seems to make sense to implement this logic as a subclass. You can find such a class – DatabaseInstaller – in the Database/Packager sample project:

```java
import android.content.Context;
import android.database.SQLException;
import android.database.sqlite.SQLiteOpenHelper;
import android.database.sqlite.SQLiteDatabase;
import android.database.sqlite.SQLiteQueryBuilder;
import java.io.*;

abstract class DatabaseInstaller extends SQLiteOpenHelper {
  abstract void handleInstallError(Throwable t);

  private Context ctxt=null;

  public DatabaseInstaller(Context context, String name,
                           SQLiteDatabase.CursorFactory factory,
                           int version) {
    super(context, name, factory, version);

    this.ctxt=context;
  }

  @Override
  public void onCreate(SQLiteDatabase db) {
    try {
      InputStream stream=ctxt
                       .getResources()
                       .openRawResource(R.raw.packaged_db);
      InputStreamReader is=new InputStreamReader(stream);
      BufferedReader in=new BufferedReader(is);
      String str;

      while ((str = in.readLine()) != null) {
        if (!str.equals("BEGIN TRANSACTION;") && !str.equals("COMMIT;")) {
          db.execSQL(str);
        }
      }

      in.close();
    }
    catch (IOException e) {
      handleInstallError(e);
    }
```

Databases and Content Providers

```
  }
}
```

This class is abstract, expecting subclasses to implement both the `onUpgrade()` path from `SQLiteOpenHelper` and a `handleInstallError()` callback in case something fails during `onCreate()`.

Most of the smarts are found in `DatabaseInstaller`'s `onCreate()` implementation. Since `SQLiteDatabase` has no means to execute SQL statements contained in an `InputStream`, we are stuck opening the `R.raw.packaged_db` resource and reading the statements out ourselves, one at a time.

However, the exported SQL will likely contain `BEGIN TRANSACTION;` and `COMMIT;` statements, since `sqlite3` expects that `sqlite3` itself would be used to re-executed the dumped SQL script. Since transactions are handled via API calls with `SQLiteDatabase`, we cannot execute `BEGIN TRANSACTION;` and `COMMIT;` statements via `execSQL()` without getting a "nested transaction" error. So, we skip those two statements and execute everything else, one line at a time.

The net result: `onCreate()` takes our raw SQL and turns it into a table in our on-device database.

Of course, to really use this, you will need to create a `DatabaseInstaller` subclass, such as `ConstantsInstaller`:

```
import android.content.Context;
import android.database.sqlite.SQLiteDatabase;
import android.util.Log;

class ConstantsInstaller  extends DatabaseInstaller {
  public ConstantsInstaller(Context context, String name,
                            SQLiteDatabase.CursorFactory factory,
                            int version)  {
    super(context, name, factory, version);
  }

  void handleInstallError(Throwable t) {
    Log.e("Constants", "Exception installing database", t);
```

```
    }
    @Override
    public void onUpgrade(SQLiteDatabase db, int oldVersion,
                          int newVersion) {
      db.execSQL("DROP TABLE IF EXISTS constants");
      onCreate(db);
    }
}
```

The rest of this project is largely identical to the ContentProvider/Constants sample from *The Busy Coder's Guide to Android Development*.

One possible enhancement to DatabaseInstaller is to create our own transaction around the loop of execSQL() calls. This would improve performance dramatically, as otherwise, each execSQL() call is its own transaction. The proof of this is left to the reader as an exercise.

Examining Your Relationships

Android has a built-in contact manager, integrated with the phone dialer. You can work with the contacts via the Contacts content provider.

However, compared to content providers found in, say, simplified book examples, the Contacts content provider is rather intimidating. After all, there are 16 classes and 9 interfaces all involved in accessing this content provider. This section will attempt to illustrate some of the patterns for making use of Contacts.

Contact Permissions

Since contacts are privileged data, you need certain permissions to work with them. Specifically, you need the READ_CONTACTS permission to query and examine the Contacts content and WRITE_CONTACTS to add, modify, or remove contacts from the system.

For example, here is the manifest for the Database/Contacts sample application:

Databases and Content Providers

```xml
<?xml version="1.0" encoding="utf-8"?>
<manifest xmlns:android="http://schemas.android.com/apk/res/android"
    package="com.commonsware.android.database"
    android:versionCode="1"
    android:versionName="1.0">
  <uses-permission android:name="android.permission.READ_CONTACTS" />
    <application android:label="@string/app_name">
        <activity android:name=".ContactsDemo"
                  android:label="@string/app_name">
            <intent-filter>
                <action android:name="android.intent.action.MAIN" />
                <category android:name="android.intent.category.LAUNCHER" />
            </intent-filter>
        </activity>
    </application>
</manifest>
```

Pre-Joined Data

While the database underlying the `Contacts` content provider is private, one can imagine that it has several tables: one for people, one for their phone numbers, one for their email addresses, etc. These are tied together by typical database relations, most likely 1:N, so the phone number and email address tables would have a foreign key pointing back to the table containing information about people.

To simplify accessing all of this through the content provider interface, Android pre-joins queries against some of the tables. For example, one can query for phone numbers and get the contact name and other data along with the number, without having to somehow do a join operation yourself.

The Sample Activity

The `ContactsDemo` activity is simply a `ListActivity`, though it sports a `Spinner` to go along with the obligatory `ListView`:

```xml
<?xml version="1.0" encoding="utf-8"?>
<LinearLayout xmlns:android="http://schemas.android.com/apk/res/android"
    android:orientation="vertical"
    android:layout_width="fill_parent"
    android:layout_height="fill_parent"
    >
  <Spinner android:id="@+id/spinner"
```

Databases and Content Providers

```
      android:layout_width="fill_parent"
      android:layout_height="wrap_content"
      android:drawSelectorOnTop="true"
  />
  <ListView
      android:id="@android:id/list"
      android:layout_width="fill_parent"
      android:layout_height="fill_parent"
      android:drawSelectorOnTop="false"
  />
</LinearLayout>
```

The activity itself sets up a listener on the Spinner and toggles the list of information shown in the ListView when the Spinner value changes:

```
package com.commonsware.android.database;

import android.app.ListActivity;
import android.database.Cursor;
import android.os.Bundle;
import android.provider.Contacts;
import android.view.View;
import android.widget.AdapterView;
import android.widget.ArrayAdapter;
import android.widget.ListAdapter;
import android.widget.SimpleCursorAdapter;
import android.widget.Spinner;

public class ContactsDemo extends ListActivity
  implements AdapterView.OnItemSelectedListener {
  private static String[] options={"Contact Names",
                                   "Contact Names & Numbers",
                                   "Contact Names & Email Addresses"};
  private ListAdapter[] listAdapters=new ListAdapter[3];

  @Override
  public void onCreate(Bundle savedInstanceState) {
    super.onCreate(savedInstanceState);
    setContentView(R.layout.main);

    initListAdapters();

    Spinner spin=(Spinner)findViewById(R.id.spinner);
    spin.setOnItemSelectedListener(this);

    ArrayAdapter<String> aa=new ArrayAdapter<String>(this,
                    android.R.layout.simple_spinner_item,
                    options);

    aa.setDropDownViewResource(
            android.R.layout.simple_spinner_dropdown_item);
    spin.setAdapter(aa);
```

Databases and Content Providers

```java
  }
  public void onItemSelected(AdapterView<?> parent,
                             View v, int position, long id) {
    setListAdapter(listAdapters[position]);
  }

  public void onNothingSelected(AdapterView<?> parent) {
    // ignore
  }
  private void initListAdapters() {
    listAdapters[0]=buildNameAdapter();
    listAdapters[1]=buildPhonesAdapter();
    listAdapters[2]=buildEmailAdapter();
  }

  private ListAdapter buildNameAdapter() {
    String[] PROJECTION=new String[] { Contacts.People._ID,
                                       Contacts.PeopleColumns.NAME
                                     };
    Cursor c=managedQuery(Contacts.People.CONTENT_URI,
                          PROJECTION, null, null,
                          Contacts.People.DEFAULT_SORT_ORDER);

    return(new SimpleCursorAdapter( this,
                                    android.R.layout.simple_list_item_1,
                                    c,
                                    new String[] {
                                      Contacts.PeopleColumns.NAME
                                    },
                                    new int[] {
                                      android.R.id.text1
                                    }));
  }

  private ListAdapter buildPhonesAdapter() {
    String[] PROJECTION=new String[] { Contacts.Phones._ID,
                                       Contacts.Phones.NAME,
                                       Contacts.Phones.NUMBER
                                     };
    Cursor c=managedQuery(Contacts.Phones.CONTENT_URI,
                          PROJECTION, null, null,
                          Contacts.Phones.DEFAULT_SORT_ORDER);

    return(new SimpleCursorAdapter( this,
                                    android.R.layout.simple_list_item_2,
                                    c,
                                    new String[] {
                                      Contacts.Phones.NAME,
                                      Contacts.Phones.NUMBER
                                    },
                                    new int[] {
                                      android.R.id.text1,
```

```
                                    android.R.id.text2
                                }));
}
private ListAdapter buildEmailAdapter() {
  String[] PROJECTION=new String[] { Contacts.ContactMethods._ID,
                                Contacts.ContactMethods.DATA,
                                Contacts.PeopleColumns.NAME
                              };
  Cursor c=managedQuery(Contacts.ContactMethods.CONTENT_EMAIL_URI,
                 PROJECTION, null, null,
                 Contacts.ContactMethods.DEFAULT_SORT_ORDER);

  return(new SimpleCursorAdapter(  this,
                                android.R.layout.simple_list_item_2,
                                c,
                                new String[] {
                                  Contacts.PeopleColumns.NAME,
                                  Contacts.ContactMethods.DATA
                                },
                                new int[] {
                                  android.R.id.text1,
                                  android.R.id.text2
                                }));
  }
}
```

When the activity is first opened, it sets up three Adapter objects, one for each of three perspectives on the contacts data. The Spinner simply resets the list to use the Adapter associated with the Spinner value selected.

Accessing People

The first Adapter shows the names of all of the contacts. Since all the information we seek is in the contact itself, we can use the CONTENT_URI provider, retrieve all of the contacts in the default sort order, and pour them into a SimpleCursorAdapter set up to show each person on its own row:

```
private ListAdapter buildNameAdapter() {
  String[] PROJECTION=new String[] { Contacts.People._ID,
                                Contacts.PeopleColumns.NAME
                              };
  Cursor c=managedQuery(Contacts.People.CONTENT_URI,
                 PROJECTION, null, null,
                 Contacts.People.DEFAULT_SORT_ORDER);

  return(new SimpleCursorAdapter(  this,
                                android.R.layout.simple_list_item_1,
```

Databases and Content Providers

```
                            c,
                            new String[] {
                              Contacts.PeopleColumns.NAME
                            },
                            new int[] {
                              android.R.id.text1
                            }));
}
```

Assuming you have some contacts in the database, they will appear when you first open the ContactsDemo activity, since that is the default perspective:

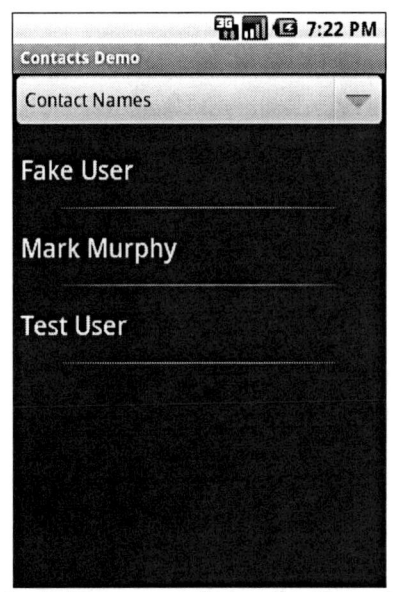

Figure 37. The ContactsDemo sample application, showing all contacts

Accessing Phone Numbers

Retrieving a list of contacts by their phone number can be done by querying the CONTENT_URI content provider:

```
private ListAdapter buildPhonesAdapter() {
  String[] PROJECTION=new String[] { Contacts.Phones._ID,
                                     Contacts.Phones.NAME,
                                     Contacts.Phones.NUMBER
                                   };
  Cursor c=managedQuery(Contacts.Phones.CONTENT_URI,
                        PROJECTION, null, null,
```

```
                    Contacts.Phones.DEFAULT_SORT_ORDER);

  return(new SimpleCursorAdapter(  this,
                                   android.R.layout.simple_list_item_2,
                                   c,
                                   new String[] {
                                     Contacts.Phones.NAME,
                                     Contacts.Phones.NUMBER
                                   },
                                   new int[] {
                                     android.R.id.text1,
                                     android.R.id.text2
                                   }));
}
```

Since the documentation for Contacts.Phones shows that it incorporates Contacts.PeopleColumns and Contacts.PhonesColumns, we know we can get the phone number and the contact's name in one query, which is why both are included in our projection of columns to retrieve.

Figure 38. The ContactsDemo sample application, showing all contacts that have phone numbers

Accessing Email Addresses

Similarly, to get a list of all the email addresses, we can use the `CONTENT_EMAIL_URI` content provider, which incorporates the `Contacts.ContactMethodsColumns` and `Contacts.PeopleColumns`, so we can get access to the contact name as well as the email address itself (DATA):

```
private ListAdapter buildEmailAdapter() {
  String[] PROJECTION=new String[] { Contacts.ContactMethods._ID,
                                     Contacts.ContactMethods.DATA,
                                     Contacts.PeopleColumns.NAME
                                   };
  Cursor c=managedQuery(Contacts.ContactMethods.CONTENT_EMAIL_URI,
                        PROJECTION, null, null,
                        Contacts.ContactMethods.DEFAULT_SORT_ORDER);

  return(new SimpleCursorAdapter( this,
                                  android.R.layout.simple_list_item_2,
                                  c,
                                  new String[] {
                                    Contacts.PeopleColumns.NAME,
                                    Contacts.ContactMethods.DATA
                                  },
                                  new int[] {
                                    android.R.id.text1,
                                    android.R.id.text2
                                  }));
}
```

Again, the results are displayed via a two-line `SimpleCursorAdapter`:

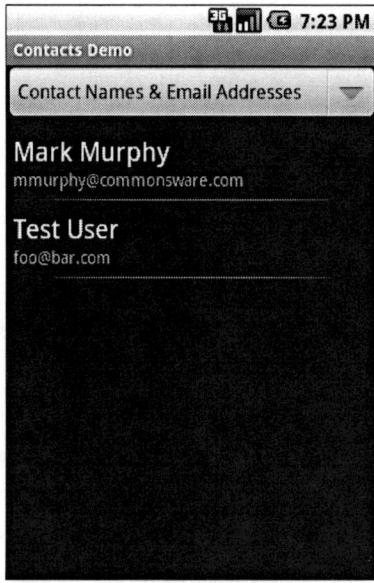

Figure 39. The ContactsDemo sample application, showing all contacts with email addresses

Rummaging Through Your Phone Records

The `CallLog` content provider in Android gives you access to the calls associated with your phone: the calls you placed, the calls you received, and the calls that you missed. This is a much simpler structure than the `Contacts` content provider described in the previous section.

The columns available to you can be found in the `CallLog.Calls` class. The commonly-used ones include:

- `NUMBER`: the phone number associated with the call
- `DATE`: when the call was placed, in milliseconds-since-the-epoch format
- `DURATION`: how long the call lasted, in seconds
- `TYPE`: indicating if the call was incoming, outgoing, or missed

These, of course, are augmented by the stock `BaseColumns`, which `CallLog.Calls` inherits from.

So, for example, here is a projection used against the call log, from the `JoinDemo` activity in the `Database/JoinCursor` project:

```
private static String[] PROJECTION=new String[] { CallLog.Calls._ID,
                                                  CallLog.Calls.NUMBER,
                                                  CallLog.Calls.DATE,
                                                  CallLog.Calls.DURATION
                                                };
```

Here is where we get a `Cursor` on that projection, with the most-recent calls first in the list:

```
Cursor c=managedQuery(android.provider.CallLog.Calls.CONTENT_URI,
                      PROJECTION, null, null,
                      CallLog.Calls.DATE+" DESC");
```

Unlike contacts, the call log appears unmodifiable by Android applications. So while you can query the log, you cannot add your own calls, delete calls, etc.

Also note that, to access the call log, you need the `READ_CONTACTS` permission.

Come Together, Right Now

If you have multiple tables within a database, and you want a `Cursor` that represents a join of those tables, you can accomplish that simply through a well-constructed query. However, if you have multiple databases, or you wish to join data in your database with data from a third-party `ContentProvider`, the join becomes significantly more difficult. You cannot simply construct a query, since SQLite has no facility (today) to query a `ContentProvider`, let alone join a `ContentProvider`'s contents with those from native tables.

One solution is to do the join at the `Cursor` itself. Android's `Cursors` offer a fairly vanilla interface, and Android even supplies a `CursorWrapper` class that can handle much of the effort for us. In this section, we will examine the use of `CursorWrapper` to create a `JoinCursor`, blending data from a SQLite table with that from the `CallLog`.

Note that the implementation shown here is for illustrative purposes only. It may suffer from significant performance issues, particularly memory consumption, that would need to be addressed in a serious production application. If you are interested in perhaps pursuing an open source project to implement a better version of `JoinCursor`, contact the author[24].

Also note that there is a `CursorJoiner` class in the `android.database` package in the SDK. A `CursorJoiner` takes two `Cursor` objects plus a list of key columns, using the key columns to join the `Cursor` values together. This is more efficient but somewhat less flexible that the implemenation shown here.

CursorWrapper

As the name suggests, `CursorWrapper` wraps a `Cursor` object. Specifically, `CursorWrapper` implements the `Cursor` interface itself and delegates all of the interface's calls to the wrapped `Cursor`.

On the surface, this seems pointless. After all, if `CursorWrapper` simply serves as a pass-through to the `Cursor`, why not use the underlying `Cursor` directly?

The key is not `CursorWrapper` itself, but rather custom subclasses of `CursorWrapper`. You can then override certain `Cursor` methods, to perform work in addition to, or perhaps instead of, passing the call to the wrapped `Cursor`.

In this case, we want to create a `CursorWrapper` subclass that allows us to inject additional columns into the results. These columns will be the result of a join operation between a SQLite table and the `CallLog`.

---

24 mailto:mmurphy@commonsware.com

Databases and Content Providers

Specifically, the Database/JoinCursor project adds "call notes" – a block of text about a specific call one made. You could use this concept in a contact management system, for example, to annotate what all was discussed in a call or otherwise document the call itself. Since `CallLog` is not modifiable and has no field for "call notes" anyway, we cannot store such notes in the `CallLog`. Instead, we store those notes in a call_notes SQLite table, mapping the `CallLog` row `_id` to the note.

For simplicity, this example will assume that there are 0 or 1 notes per call, not several. That allows the `JoinCursor` to simply inject the call note into the `CallLog` `Cursor` results, without having to worry about dealing with several possible notes. We do, however, need to deal with the case where the call does not yet have a note.

Implementing a JoinCursor

A `JoinCursor` is a relatively complex class. Some of that complexity is due to repeated boilerplate code, and some is due to the problem being solved.

What we need the `JoinCursor` to do is:

- Override `Cursor`-related methods that involve the columns
- Check to see if there is a note for the current row
- Adjust the results of the method to accomodate the possibility (or reality) of a note

You can see an implementation of this in the `JoinCursor` class in the `Database/JoinCursor` project:

```
import android.content.ContentValues;
import android.database.Cursor;
import android.database.CursorWrapper;
import java.util.LinkedHashMap;
import java.util.Map;

class JoinCursor extends CursorWrapper {
  private I_JoinHandler join=null;
  private JoinCache cache=new JoinCache(100);
```

Databases and Content Providers

```java
JoinCursor(Cursor main, I_JoinHandler join) {
  super(main);

  this.join=join;
}

public int getColumnCount() {
  return(super.getColumnCount()+join.getColumnNames().length);
}

public int getColumnIndex(String columnName) {
  for (int i=0;i<join.getColumnNames().length;i++) {
    if (columnName.equals(join.getColumnNames()[i])) {
      return(super.getColumnCount()+i);
    }
  }

  return(super.getColumnIndex(columnName));
}

public int getColumnIndexOrThrow(String columnName) {
  for (int i=0;i<join.getColumnNames().length;i++) {
    if (columnName.equals(join.getColumnNames()[i])) {
      return(super.getColumnCount()+i);
    }
  }

  return(super.getColumnIndexOrThrow(columnName));
}

public String getColumnName(int columnIndex) {
  if (columnIndex>=super.getColumnCount()) {
    return(join.getColumnNames()[columnIndex-super.getColumnCount()]);
  }

  return(super.getColumnName(columnIndex));
}

public byte[] getBlob(int columnIndex) {
  if (columnIndex>=super.getColumnCount()) {
    ContentValues extras=cache.get(join.getCacheKey(this));
    int offset=columnIndex-super.getColumnCount();

    return(extras.getAsByteArray(join.getColumnNames()[offset]));
  }

  return(super.getBlob(columnIndex));
}

public double getDouble(int columnIndex) {
  if (columnIndex>=super.getColumnCount()) {
    ContentValues extras=cache.get(join.getCacheKey(this));
    int offset=columnIndex-super.getColumnCount();

    return(extras.getAsDouble(join.getColumnNames()[offset]));
```

Databases and Content Providers

```java
    }

    return(super.getDouble(columnIndex));
  }

  public float getFloat(int columnIndex) {
    if (columnIndex>=super.getColumnCount()) {
      ContentValues extras=cache.get(join.getCacheKey(this));
      int offset=columnIndex-super.getColumnCount();

      return(extras.getAsFloat(join.getColumnNames()[offset]));
    }

    return(super.getFloat(columnIndex));
  }

  public int getInt(int columnIndex) {
    if (columnIndex>=super.getColumnCount()) {
      ContentValues extras=cache.get(join.getCacheKey(this));
      int offset=columnIndex-super.getColumnCount();

      return(extras.getAsInteger(join.getColumnNames()[offset]));
    }

    return(super.getInt(columnIndex));
  }

  public long getLong(int columnIndex) {
    if (columnIndex>=super.getColumnCount()) {
      ContentValues extras=cache.get(join.getCacheKey(this));
      int offset=columnIndex-super.getColumnCount();

      return(extras.getAsLong(join.getColumnNames()[offset]));
    }

    return(super.getLong(columnIndex));
  }

  public short getShort(int columnIndex) {
    if (columnIndex>=super.getColumnCount()) {
      ContentValues extras=cache.get(join.getCacheKey(this));
      int offset=columnIndex-super.getColumnCount();

      return(extras.getAsShort(join.getColumnNames()[offset]));
    }

    return(super.getShort(columnIndex));
  }

  public String getString(int columnIndex) {
    if (columnIndex>=super.getColumnCount()) {
      ContentValues extras=cache.get(join.getCacheKey(this));
      int offset=columnIndex-super.getColumnCount();

      return(extras.getAsString(join.getColumnNames()[offset]));
```

```
    }

    return(super.getString(columnIndex));
  }

  public boolean isNull(int columnIndex) {
    if (columnIndex>=super.getColumnCount()) {
      ContentValues extras=cache.get(join.getCacheKey(this));
      int offset=columnIndex-super.getColumnCount();

      return(extras.get(join.getColumnNames()[offset])==null);
    }

    return(super.isNull(columnIndex));
  }

  public boolean requery() {
    cache.clear();

    return(super.requery());
  }

  class JoinCache extends LinkedHashMap<String, ContentValues> {
    private int capacity=100;

    JoinCache(int capacity) {
      super(capacity+1, 1.1f, true);
      this.capacity=capacity;
    }

    protected boolean removeEldestEntry(Entry<String, ContentValues> eldest) {
      return(size()>capacity);
    }

    ContentValues get(String key) {
      ContentValues result=super.get(key);

      if (result==null) {
        result=join.getJoin(JoinCursor.this);
        put(key, result);
      }

      return(result);
    }
  }
}
```

JoinCursor, when instantiated, gets both the Cursor to wrap and an I_JoinHandler instance. The join handler is responsible for getting the extra columns for a given row:

Databases and Content Providers

```java
import android.content.ContentValues;
import android.database.Cursor;
import java.util.Map;

public interface I_JoinHandler {
  String[] getColumnNames();
  String getCacheKey(Cursor c);
  ContentValues getJoin(Cursor c);
}
```

Most of `JoinCursor` is then using the `I_JoinHandler` information to adjust the results of various `Cursor` methods. For example:

- `getColumnCount()` returns the sum of the `Cursor`'s column count and the number of extra columns returned by the join handler
- `getColumnIndex()` and kin need to search through the join handler's columns as well as the `Cursor`'s to find the match, if any
- `getInt()`, `isNull()`, and kin need to support retrieving values from both the `Cursor` and the join handler

To improve performance, `JoinCursor` keeps a cache of the extra values for requested rows, using an "LRU cache"-style `LinkedHashMap` and an inner `JoinCache` class. The `JoinCache` keeps the `ContentValues` returned by `I_JoinHandler` on a `getJoin()` call, representing the extra columns (if any) for that particular `Cursor` row. Since we are caching data, however, we need to flush that cache sometimes; in this case, we override `requery()` to flush the cache if the `Cursor` itself is being proactively updated.

Using a JoinCursor

To use a `JoinCursor`, of course, you need an implementation of `I_JoinHandler`, such as this one from the `JoinDemo` activity:

```java
I_JoinHandler join=new I_JoinHandler() {
  String[] columns={NOTE_ID, NOTE};

  public String[] getColumnNames() {
      return(columns);
  }

  public String getCacheKey(Cursor c) {
      return(String.valueOf(c.getInt(c.getColumnIndex(CallLog.Calls._ID))));
```

Databases and Content Providers

```
  }

  public ContentValues getJoin(Cursor c) {
    String[] args={getCacheKey(c)};
    Cursor j=getDb().rawQuery("SELECT _ID, note FROM call_notes WHERE call_id=?", args);
    ContentValues result=new ContentValues();

    j.moveToFirst();

    if (j.isAfterLast()) {
      result.put(columns[0], -1);
      result.put(columns[1], (String)null);
    }
    else {
      result.put(columns[0], j.getInt(0));
      result.put(columns[1], j.getString(1));
    }

    j.close();

    return(result);
  }
};
```

The columns are a fixed pair (the note's ID and the note itself). These are retrieved via `getJoin()` from the `call_notes` SQLite table. The call notes themselves are keyed by the call's own `_id`, which is also used as the key for the `JoinCursor`'s cache of results. The net effect is that we only ever retrieve a note once for a given call, at least until a `requery()`. And, if there is no note for the call, we use a `null` note to indicate that we are, indeed, note-free for this call.

The note information is then used by our `CursorAdapter` subclass (`CallPlusAdapter`) and its associated `ViewWrapper`, also found in the `JoinDemo` activity:

```
class CallPlusAdapter extends CursorAdapter {
  CallPlusAdapter(Cursor c) {
    super(JoinDemo.this, c);
  }

  @Override
  public void bindView(View row, Context ctxt,
                       Cursor c) {
    ViewWrapper wrapper=(ViewWrapper)row.getTag();

    wrapper.update(c);
```

Databases and Content Providers

```java
  }

  @Override
  public View newView(Context ctxt, Cursor c,
                     ViewGroup parent) {
    LayoutInflater inflater=getLayoutInflater();

    View row=inflater.inflate(R.layout.row, null);
    ViewWrapper wrapper=new ViewWrapper(row);

    row.setTag(wrapper);
    wrapper.update(c);

    return(row);
  }
}

class ViewWrapper {
  View base;
  TextView number=null;
  TextView duration=null;
  TextView time=null;
  ImageView icon=null;

  ViewWrapper(View base) {
    this.base=base;
  }

  TextView getNumber() {
    if (number==null) {
      number=(TextView)base.findViewById(R.id.number);
    }

    return(number);
  }

  TextView getDuration() {
    if (duration==null) {
      duration=(TextView)base.findViewById(R.id.duration);
    }

    return(duration);
  }

  TextView getTime() {
    if (time==null) {
      time=(TextView)base.findViewById(R.id.time);
    }

    return(time);
  }

  ImageView getIcon() {
    if (icon==null) {
```

```
      icon=(ImageView)base.findViewById(R.id.note);
    }

    return(icon);
  }

  void update(Cursor c) {
    getNumber().setText(c.getString(c.getColumnIndex(CallLog.Calls.NUMBER)));
    getTime().setText(FORMAT.format(c.getInt(c.getColumnIndex(CallLog.Calls.DATE
)))));
    getDuration().setText(c.getString(c.getColumnIndex(CallLog.Calls.DURATION))
+" seconds");

    String note=c.getString(c.getColumnIndex(NOTE));

    if (note!=null && note.length()>0) {
      getIcon().setVisibility(View.VISIBLE);
    }
    else {
      getIcon().setVisibility(View.GONE);
    }
  }
}
```

Mostly, we are populating a row to go in a ListView based off of the call data (e.g., duration). However, if there is a non-null note, we also display an icon in the row, indicating that a note is available.

The JoinDemo activity itself is just a ListActivity, using the CallPlusAdapter and the CallLog Cursor we saw in the previous section:

```
import android.app.ListActivity;
import android.content.ContentValues;
import android.content.Context;
import android.content.Intent;
import android.database.Cursor;
import android.database.sqlite.SQLiteDatabase;
import android.os.Bundle;
import android.provider.CallLog;
import android.view.View;
import android.view.ViewGroup;
import android.view.LayoutInflater;
import android.widget.CursorAdapter;
import android.widget.ImageView;
import android.widget.ListView;
import android.widget.TextView;
import java.text.SimpleDateFormat;

public class JoinDemo extends ListActivity {
  public static String NOTE=" NOTE";
```

Databases and Content Providers

```java
private static String NOTE_ID="NOTE_ID";
private static String[] PROJECTION=new String[] { CallLog.Calls._ID,
                                                  CallLog.Calls.NUMBER,
                                                  CallLog.Calls.DATE,
                                                  CallLog.Calls.DURATION
                                                };
private static SimpleDateFormat FORMAT=new SimpleDateFormat("MM/d h:mm a");
private Cursor cursor=null;
private int noteColumn=-1;
private int idColumn=-1;
private int noteIdColumn=-1;
private SQLiteDatabase db=null;

@Override
public void onCreate(Bundle savedInstanceState) {
  super.onCreate(savedInstanceState);

  Cursor c=managedQuery(android.provider.CallLog.Calls.CONTENT_URI,
                        PROJECTION, null, null,
                        CallLog.Calls.DATE+" DESC");

  cursor=new JoinCursor(c, join);
  noteColumn=cursor.getColumnIndex(NOTE);
  idColumn=cursor.getColumnIndex(CallLog.Calls._ID);
  noteIdColumn=cursor.getColumnIndex(NOTE_ID);
  setListAdapter(new CallPlusAdapter(cursor));
}

@Override
public void onResume() {
  super.onResume();

  cursor.requery();
}

@Override
public void onDestroy() {
  super.onDestroy();

  if (db!=null) {
    db.close();
  }
}

@Override
protected void onListItemClick(ListView l, View v,
                               int position, long id) {
  cursor.moveToPosition(position);

  String note=cursor.getString(noteColumn);

  if (note==null || note.length()==0) {
    Intent i=new Intent(this, NoteEditor.class);

    i.putExtra(NOTE, note);
```

Databases and Content Providers

```java
      i.putExtra("call_id", cursor.getInt(idColumn));
      i.putExtra("note_id", cursor.getInt(noteIdColumn));
      startActivityForResult(i, 1);
    }
    else {
      Intent i=new Intent(this, NoteActivity.class);

      i.putExtra(NOTE, note);
      startActivity(i);
    }
  }

  @Override
  protected void onActivityResult(int requestCode,
                                  int resultCode,
                                  Intent data) {
    String note=data.getStringExtra(NOTE);

    if (note!=null) {
      int noteId=data.getIntExtra(NOTE_ID, -1);
      ContentValues cv=new ContentValues();

      cv.put("note", note);

      if (noteId==-1) {
        int callId=data.getIntExtra("call_id", -1);

        cv.put("call_id", callId);

        getDb().insertOrThrow("call_notes", "_id", cv);
      }
      else {
        String[] args={String.valueOf(noteId)};

        getDb().update("call_notes", cv, "_ID", args);
      }
    }
  }

  SQLiteDatabase getDb() {
    if (db==null) {
      db=(new NotesInstaller(JoinDemo.this)).getWritableDatabase();
    }

    return(db);
  }

  I_JoinHandler join=new I_JoinHandler() {
    String[] columns={NOTE_ID, NOTE};

    public String[] getColumnNames() {
      return(columns);
    }

    public String getCacheKey(Cursor c) {
```

Databases and Content Providers

```
      return(String.valueOf(c.getInt(c.getColumnIndex(CallLog.Calls._ID))));
    }

    public ContentValues getJoin(Cursor c) {
      String[] args={getCacheKey(c)};
      Cursor j=getDb().rawQuery("SELECT _ID, note FROM call_notes WHERE call_id=?", args);
      ContentValues result=new ContentValues();

      j.moveToFirst();

      if (j.isAfterLast()) {
        result.put(columns[0], -1);
        result.put(columns[1], (String)null);
      }
      else {
        result.put(columns[0], j.getInt(0));
        result.put(columns[1], j.getString(1));
      }

      j.close();

      return(result);
    }
  };

  class CallPlusAdapter extends CursorAdapter {
    CallPlusAdapter(Cursor c) {
      super(JoinDemo.this, c);
    }

    @Override
    public void bindView(View row, Context ctxt,
                         Cursor c) {
      ViewWrapper wrapper=(ViewWrapper)row.getTag();

      wrapper.update(c);
    }

    @Override
    public View newView(Context ctxt, Cursor c,
                        ViewGroup parent) {
      LayoutInflater inflater=getLayoutInflater();

      View row=inflater.inflate(R.layout.row, null);
      ViewWrapper wrapper=new ViewWrapper(row);

      row.setTag(wrapper);
      wrapper.update(c);

      return(row);
    }
  }

  class ViewWrapper {
```

```java
    View base;
    TextView number=null;
    TextView duration=null;
    TextView time=null;
    ImageView icon=null;

    ViewWrapper(View base) {
      this.base=base;
    }

    TextView getNumber() {
      if (number==null) {
        number=(TextView)base.findViewById(R.id.number);
      }

      return(number);
    }

    TextView getDuration() {
      if (duration==null) {
        duration=(TextView)base.findViewById(R.id.duration);
      }

      return(duration);
    }

    TextView getTime() {
      if (time==null) {
        time=(TextView)base.findViewById(R.id.time);
      }

      return(time);
    }

    ImageView getIcon() {
      if (icon==null) {
        icon=(ImageView)base.findViewById(R.id.note);
      }

      return(icon);
    }

    void update(Cursor c) {
      getNumber().setText(c.getString(c.getColumnIndex(CallLog.Calls.NUMBER)));
      getTime().setText(FORMAT.format(c.getInt(c.getColumnIndex(CallLog.Calls.DATE))));
      getDuration().setText(c.getString(c.getColumnIndex(CallLog.Calls.DURATION))+" seconds");

      String note=c.getString(c.getColumnIndex(NOTE));

      if (note!=null && note.length()>0) {
        getIcon().setVisibility(View.VISIBLE);
      }
```

Databases and Content Providers

```
    else {
      getIcon().setVisibility(View.GONE);
    }
  }
 }
}
```

When the user clicks on a row, depending on whether there is a note, we either spawn a NoteEditor (to create a new note) or a NoteActivity (to view an existing note). In a real implementation of this functionality, of course, we would allow users to edit existing notes, delete notes, and the like, all of which is skipped in this simplified sample application.

Visually, the activity does not look like much, but you will see the note icon on calls containing notes (with some phone numbers smudged for privacy):

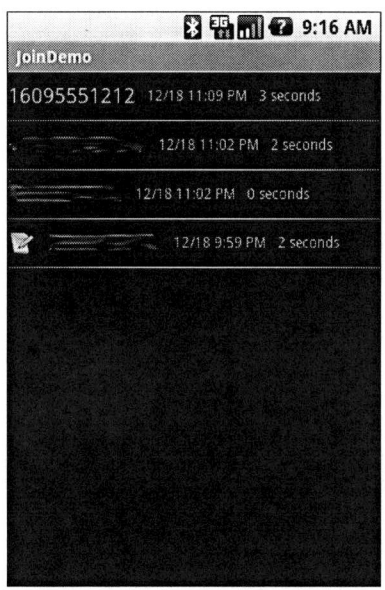

Figure 40. The JoinCursor sample application, showing one call with a note

CHAPTER 11
Handling System Events

If you have ever looked at the list of available Intent actions in the SDK documentation for the Intent class, you will see that there are lots of possible actions.

Lots and lots and lots of possible actions.

There are even actions that are not listed in that spot in the documentation, but are scattered throughout the rest of the SDK documentation.

The vast majority of these you will never raise yourself. Instead, they are broadcast by Android, to signify certain system events that have occurred and that you might want to take note of, if they affect the operation of your application.

This chapter examines a few of these, to give you the sense of what is possible and how to make use of these sorts of events.

Get Moving, First Thing

A popular request is to have a service get control when the device is powered on.

Handling System Events

This is doable but somewhat dangerous, in that too many on-boot requests slow down the device startup and may make things sluggish for the user. Moreover, the more services that are running all the time, the worse the device performance will be.

A better pattern is to get control on boot to arrange for a service to do something periodically using the `AlarmManager` or via other system events. In this section, we will examine the on-boot portion of the problem – in the next chapter, we will investigate `AlarmManager` and how it can keep services active yet not necessarily resident in memory all the time.

The Permission

In order to be notified when the device has completed is system boot process, you will need to request the `RECEIVE_BOOT_COMPLETED` permission. Without this, even if you arrange to receive the boot broadcast Intent, it will not be dispatched to your receiver.

As the Android documentation describes it:

> *Though holding this permission does not have any security implications, it can have a negative impact on the user experience by increasing the amount of time it takes the system to start and allowing applications to have themselves running without the user being aware of them. As such, you must explicitly declare your use of this facility to make that visible to the user.*

The Receiver Element

There are two ways you can receive a broadcast `Intent`. One is to use `registerReceiver()` from an existing `Activity`, `Service`, or `ContentProvider`. The other is to register your interest in the `Intent` in the manifest in the form of a `<receiver>` element:

Handling System Events

```xml
<?xml version="1.0" encoding="utf-8"?>
<manifest xmlns:android="http://schemas.android.com/apk/res/android"
    package="com.commonsware.android.sysevents.boot"
    android:versionCode="1"
    android:versionName="1.0">
  <uses-permission android:name="android.permission.RECEIVE_BOOT_COMPLETED" />
    <application android:label="@string/app_name">
        <receiver android:name=".OnBootReceiver">
            <intent-filter>
                <action android:name="android.intent.action.BOOT_COMPLETED" />
            </intent-filter>
        </receiver>
    </application>
</manifest>
```

The above `AndroidManifest.xml`, from the `SystemEvents/OnBoot` sample project, shows that we have registered a broadcast receiver named `OnBootReceiver`, set to be given control when the `android.intent.action.BOOT_COMPLETED` Intent is broadcast.

In this case, we have no choice but to implement our receiver this way – by the time any of our other components (e.g., an `Activity`) were to get control and be able to call `registerReceiver()`, the `BOOT_COMPLETED` Intent will be long gone.

The Receiver Implementation

Now that we have told Android that we would like to be notified when the boot has completed, and given that we have been granted permission to do so by the user, we now need to actually do something to receive the Intent. This is a simple matter of creating a `BroadcastReceiver`, such as seen in the `OnBootCompleted` implementation shown below:

```java
package com.commonsware.android.sysevents.boot;

import android.content.BroadcastReceiver;
import android.content.Context;
import android.content.Intent;
import android.util.Log;

public class OnBootReceiver extends BroadcastReceiver {
  @Override
  public void onReceive(Context context, Intent intent) {
    Log.d("OnBootReceiver", "Hi, Mom!");
```

Handling System Events

```
    }
}
```

A `BroadcastReceiver` is not a `Context`, and so it gets passed a suitable `Context` object in `onReceive()` to use for accessing resources and the like. The `onReceive()` method also is passed the `Intent` that caused our `BroadcastReceiver` to be created, in case there are "extras" we need to pull out (none in this case).

In `onReceive()`, we can do whatever we want, subject to some limitations:

1. We are not a `Context`, like an `Activity`, so we cannot modify a UI or anything such as that

2. If we want to do anything significant, it is better to delegate that logic to a service that we start from here (e.g., calling `startService()` on the supplied `Context`) rather than actually doing it here, since `BroadcastReceiver` implementations need to be fast

3. We cannot start any background threads, directly or indirectly, since the `BroadcastReceiver` gets discarded as soon as `onReceive()` returns

In this case, we simply log the fact that we got control. In the next chapter, we will see what else we can do at boot time, to ensure one of our services gets control later on as needed.

To test this, install it on an emulator (or device), shut down the emulator, then restart it.

I Sense a Connection Between Us...

Generally speaking, Android applications do not care what sort of Internet connection is being used – 3G, GPRS, WiFi, lots of trained carrier pigeons[25], or whatever. So long as there is an Internet connection, the application is happy.

---

25 http://www.faqs.org/rfcs/rfc1149.html

Handling System Events

Sometimes, though, you may specifically want WiFi. This would be true if your application is bandwidth-intensive and you want to ensure that, should WiFi stop being available, you cut back on your work so as not to consume too much 3G/GPRS bandwidth, which is usually subject to some sort of cap or metering.

There is an android.net.wifi.WIFI_STATE_CHANGED Intent that will be broadcast, as the name suggests, whenever the state of the WiFi connection changes. You can arrange to receive this broadcast and take appropriate steps within your application.

This Intent requires no special permission, unlike the BOOT_COMPLETED Intent from the previous section. Hence, all you need to do is register a BroadcastReceiver for android.net.wifi.WIFI_STATE_CHANGED, either via registerReceiver(), or via the <receiver> element in AndroidManifest.xml, such as the one shown below, from the SystemEvents/OnWiFiChange sample project:

```
<?xml version="1.0" encoding="utf-8"?>
<manifest xmlns:android="http://schemas.android.com/apk/res/android"
    package="com.commonsware.android.sysevents.wifi"
    android:versionCode="1"
    android:versionName="1.0">
  <application android:label="@string/app_name">
    <receiver android:name=".OnWiFiChangeReceiver">
      <intent-filter>
        <action android:name="android.net.wifi.WIFI_STATE_CHANGED" />
      </intent-filter>
    </receiver>
  </application>
</manifest>
```

All we do in the manifest is tell Android to create an OnWiFiChangeReceiver object when a android.net.wifi.WIFI_STATE_CHANGED Intent is broadcast, so the receiver can do something useful.

In the case of OnWiFiChangeReceiver, it examines the value of the EXTRA_WIFI_STATE "extra" in the supplied Intent and logs an appropriate message:

Handling System Events

```java
package com.commonsware.android.sysevents.wifi;

import android.content.BroadcastReceiver;
import android.content.Context;
import android.content.Intent;
import android.net.wifi.WifiManager;
import android.util.Log;

public class OnWiFiChangeReceiver extends BroadcastReceiver {
  @Override
  public void onReceive(Context context, Intent intent) {
    int state=intent.getIntExtra(WifiManager.EXTRA_WIFI_STATE, -1);
    String msg=null;

    switch (state) {
      case WifiManager.WIFI_STATE_DISABLED:
        msg="is disabled";
        break;

      case WifiManager.WIFI_STATE_DISABLING:
        msg="is disabling";
        break;

      case WifiManager.WIFI_STATE_ENABLED:
        msg="is enabled";
        break;

      case WifiManager.WIFI_STATE_ENABLING:
        msg="is enabling";
        break;

      case WifiManager.WIFI_STATE_UNKNOWN :
        msg="has an error";
        break;

      default:
        msg="is acting strangely";
        break;
    }

    if (msg!=null) {
      Log.d("OnWiFiChanged", "WiFi "+msg);
    }
  }
}
```

The EXTRA_WIFI_STATE "extra" tells you what the state has become (e.g., we are now disabling or are now disabled), so you can take appropriate steps in your application.

Note that, to test this, you will need an actual Android device, as the emulator does not specifically support simulating WiFi connections.

Feeling Drained

One theme with system events is to use them to help make your users happier by reducing your impacts on the device while the device is not in a great state. In the preceding section, we saw how you could find out when WiFi was disabled, so you might not use as much bandwidth when on 3G/GPRS. However, not every application uses so much bandwidth as to make this optimization worthwhile.

However, most applications are impacted by battery life. Dead batteries run no apps.

So whether you are implementing a battery monitor or simply want to discontinue background operations when the battery gets low, you may wish to find out how the battery is doing.

There is an `ACTION_BATTERY_CHANGED` `Intent` that gets broadcast as the battery status changes, both in terms of charge (e.g., 80% charged) and charging (e.g., the device is now plugged into AC power). You simply need to register to receive this `Intent` when it is broadcast, then take appropriate steps.

One of the limitations of `ACTION_BATTERY_CHANGED` is that you have to use `registerReceiver()` to set up a `BroadcastReceiver` to get this `Intent` when broadcast. You cannot use a manifest-declared receiver as shown in the preceding two sections.

In `SystemEvents/OnBattery`, you will find a layout containing a `ProgressBar`, a `TextView`, and an `ImageView`, to serve as a battery monitor:

```
<?xml version="1.0" encoding="utf-8"?>
<LinearLayout xmlns:android="http://schemas.android.com/apk/res/android"
  android:orientation="vertical"
  android:layout_width="fill_parent"
  android:layout_height="fill_parent"
```

Handling System Events

```
  >
  <ProgressBar android:id="@+id/bar"
    style="?android:attr/progressBarStyleHorizontal"
    android:layout_width="fill_parent"
    android:layout_height="wrap_content" />
  <LinearLayout
    android:orientation="horizontal"
    android:layout_width="fill_parent"
    android:layout_height="wrap_content"
    >
    <TextView android:id="@+id/level"
      android:layout_width="0px"
      android:layout_height="wrap_content"
      android:layout_weight="1"
      android:textSize="16pt"
    />
    <ImageView android:id="@+id/status"
      android:layout_width="0px"
      android:layout_height="wrap_content"
      android:layout_weight="1"
    />
  </LinearLayout>
</LinearLayout>
```

This layout is used by a `BatteryMonitor` activity, which registers to receive the `ACTION_BATTERY_CHANGED` Intent in `onResume()` and unregisters in `onPause()`:

```
package com.commonsware.android.sysevents.battery;

import android.app.Activity;
import android.content.BroadcastReceiver;
import android.content.Context;
import android.content.Intent;
import android.content.IntentFilter;
import android.os.Bundle;
import android.os.BatteryManager;
import android.widget.ProgressBar;
import android.widget.ImageView;
import android.widget.TextView;

public class BatteryMonitor extends Activity {
  private ProgressBar bar=null;
  private ImageView status=null;
  private TextView level=null;

  @Override
  public void onCreate(Bundle savedInstanceState) {
    super.onCreate(savedInstanceState);
    setContentView(R.layout.main);

    bar=(ProgressBar)findViewById(R.id.bar);
```

Handling System Events

```java
    status=(ImageView)findViewById(R.id.status);
    level=(TextView)findViewById(R.id.level);
  }

  @Override
  public void onResume() {
    super.onResume();

    registerReceiver(onBatteryChanged,
                    new IntentFilter(Intent.ACTION_BATTERY_CHANGED));
  }

  @Override
  public void onPause() {
    super.onPause();

    unregisterReceiver(onBatteryChanged);
  }

  BroadcastReceiver onBatteryChanged=new BroadcastReceiver() {
    public void onReceive(Context context, Intent intent) {
      int pct=100*intent.getIntExtra("level", 1)/intent.getIntExtra("scale", 1);

      bar.setProgress(pct);
      level.setText(String.valueOf(pct));

      switch(intent.getIntExtra("status", -1)) {
        case BatteryManager.BATTERY_STATUS_CHARGING:
          status.setImageResource(R.drawable.charging);
          break;

        case BatteryManager.BATTERY_STATUS_FULL:
          int plugged=intent.getIntExtra("plugged", -1);

          if (plugged==BatteryManager.BATTERY_PLUGGED_AC ||
              plugged==BatteryManager.BATTERY_PLUGGED_USB) {
            status.setImageResource(R.drawable.full);
          }
          else {
            status.setImageResource(R.drawable.unplugged);
          }
          break;

        default:
          status.setImageResource(R.drawable.unplugged);
          break;
      }
    }
  };
}
```

The key to ACTION_BATTERY_CHANGED is in the "extras". Many "extras" are packaged in the Intent, to describe the current state of the battery, such as:

Handling System Events

- `health`, which should generally be `BATTERY_HEALTH_GOOD`
- `level`, which is the proportion of battery life remaining as an integer, specified on the scale described by the scale "extra"
- `plugged`, which will indicate if the device is plugged into AC power (`BATTERY_PLUGGED_AC`) or USB power (`BATTERY_PLUGGED_USB`)
- `scale`, which indicates the maximum possible value of level (e.g., 100, indicating that level is a percentage of charge remaining)
- `status`, which will tell you if the battery is charging (`BATTERY_STATUS_CHARGING`), full (`BATTERY_STATUS_FULL`), or discharging (`BATTERY_STATUS_DISCHARGING`)
- `technology`, which indicates what sort of battery is installed (e.g., "Li-Ion")
- `temperature`, which tells you how warm the battery is, in tenths of a degree Celsius (e.g., 213 is 21.3 degrees Celsius)
- `voltage`, indicating the current voltage being delivered by the battery, in millivolts

In the case of `BatteryMonitor`, when we receive an `ACTION_BATTERY_CHANGED` Intent, we do three things:

1. We compute the percentage of battery life remaining, by dividing the level by the scale
2. We update the `ProgressBar` and `TextView` to display the battery life as a percentage
3. We display an icon, with the icon selection depending on whether we are charging (`status` is `BATTERY_STATUS_CHARGING`), full but on the charger (`status` is `BATTERY_STATUS_FULL` and `plugged` is `BATTERY_PLUGGED_AC` or `BATTERY_PLUGGED_USB`), or are not plugged in

This only really works on a device, where you can plug and unplug it, plus get a varying charge level:

Handling System Events

Figure 41. The BatteryMonitor application

CHAPTER 12

Using System Services

Android offers a number of system services, usually obtained by getSystemService() from your Activity, Service, or other Context. These are your gateway to all sorts of capabilities, from settings to volume to WiFi. Throughout the course of this book and its companion[26], we have seen several of these system services. In this chapter, we will take a look at others that may be of value to you in building compelling Android applications.

Get Alarmed

A common question when doing Android development is "where do I set up cron jobs?"

The cron utility – popular in Linux – is a way of scheduling work to be done periodically. You teach cron what to run and when to run it (e.g., weekdays at noon), and cron takes care of the rest. Since Android has a Linux kernel at its heart, one might think that cron might literally be available.

While cron itself is not, Android does have a system service named AlarmManager which fills a similar role. You give it a PendingIntent and a time (and optional a period for repeating) and it will fire off the Intent as needed. By this mechanism, you can get a similar effect to cron.

---

26 http://commonsware.com/Android/

There is one small catch, though: Android is designed to run on mobile devices, particularly ones powered by all-too-tiny batteries. If you want your periodic tasks to be run even if the device is "asleep", you will need to take a fair number of extra steps, mostly stemming around the concept of the WakeLock.

Concept of WakeLocks

Most of the time in Android, you are developing code that will run while the user is actually using the device. Activities, for example, only really make sense when the device is fully awake and the user is tapping on the screen or keyboard.

Particularly with scheduled background tasks, though, you need to bear in mind that the device will eventually "go to sleep". In full sleep mode, the display, main CPU, and keyboard are all powered off, to maximize battery life. Only on a low-level system event, like an incoming phone call, will anything wake up.

Another thing that will partially wake up the phone is an Intent raised by the AlarmManager. So long as broadcast receivers are processing that Intent, the AlarmManager ensures the CPU will be running (though the screen and keyboard are still off). Once the broadcast receivers are done, the AlarmManager lets the device go back to sleep.

You can achieve the same effect in your code via a WakeLock, obtained via the PowerManager system service. When you acquire a "partial WakeLock" (PARTIAL_WAKE_LOCK), you prevent the CPU from going back to sleep until you release said WakeLock. By proper use of a partial WakeLock, you can ensure the CPU will not get shut off while you are trying to do background work, while still allowing the device to sleep most of the time, in between alarm events.

However, using a WakeLock is a bit tricky, particularly when responding to an alarm Intent, as we will see in the next few sections.

Using System Services

Scheduling Alarms

The first step to creating a `cron` workalike is to arrange to get control when the device boots. After all, the `cron` daemon starts on boot as well, and we have no other way of ensuring that our background tasks start firing after a phone is reset.

We saw how to do that in a previous chapter – set up an `RECEIVE_BOOT_COMPLETED` `BroadcastReceiver`, with appropriate permissions. Here, for example, is the `AndroidManifest.xml` from `SystemServices/Alarm`:

```xml
<?xml version="1.0" encoding="utf-8"?>
<manifest xmlns:android="http://schemas.android.com/apk/res/android"
    package="com.commonsware.android.syssvc.alarm"
    android:versionCode="1"
    android:versionName="1.0">
  <uses-permission android:name="android.permission.RECEIVE_BOOT_COMPLETED" />
  <uses-permission android:name="android.permission.WAKE_LOCK" />
  <application android:label="@string/app_name">
    <receiver android:name=".OnBootReceiver">
      <intent-filter>
        <action android:name="android.intent.action.BOOT_COMPLETED" />
      </intent-filter>
    </receiver>
    <receiver android:name=".OnAlarmReceiver">
    </receiver>
    <service android:name=".AppService">
    </service>
  </application>
</manifest>
```

We ask for an `OnBootReceiver` to get control when the device starts up, and it is in `OnBootReceiver` that we schedule our recurring alarm:

```
package com.commonsware.android.syssvc.alarm;

import android.app.AlarmManager;
import android.app.PendingIntent;
import android.content.BroadcastReceiver;
import android.content.Context;
import android.content.Intent;
import android.os.SystemClock;
import android.util.Log;

public class OnBootReceiver extends BroadcastReceiver {
  private static final int PERIOD=300000;   // 5 minutes
```

Using System Services

```
    @Override
    public void onReceive(Context context, Intent intent) {
      AlarmManager
mgr=(AlarmManager)context.getSystemService(Context.ALARM_SERVICE);
      Intent i=new Intent(context, OnAlarmReceiver.class);
      PendingIntent pi=PendingIntent.getBroadcast(context, 0,
                                                  i, 0);

      mgr.setRepeating(AlarmManager.ELAPSED_REALTIME_WAKEUP,
                       SystemClock.elapsedRealtime(),
                       PERIOD,
                       pi);
    }
}
```

We get the `AlarmManager` via `getSystemService()`, create an `Intent` referencing another `BroadcastReceiver` (`OnAlarmReceiver`), wrap that `Intent` in a `PendingIntent`, and tell the `AlarmManager` to set up a repeating alarm via `setRepeating()`. By saying we want a `ELAPSED_REALTIME_WAKEUP` alarm, we indicate that we want the alarm to wake up the device (even if it is asleep) and to express all times using the time base used by `SystemClock.elapsedRealtime()`. In this case, our alarm is set to go off every five minutes.

This will cause the `AlarmManager` to raise our `Intent` imminently, and every five minutes thereafter.

Arranging for Work From Alarms

When an alarm goes off, our `OnAlarmReceiver` will get control. It needs to arrange for a service (in this case, named `AppService`) to do its work in the background, but then release control quickly – `onReceive()` cannot take very much time.

Here is the tiny implementation of `OnAlarmReceiver` from SystemServices/Alarm:

```
package com.commonsware.android.syssvc.alarm;

import android.content.BroadcastReceiver;
import android.content.Context;
import android.content.Intent;
```

Using System Services

```java
import android.util.Log;

public class OnAlarmReceiver extends BroadcastReceiver {
  @Override
  public void onReceive(Context context, Intent intent) {
    WakefulIntentService.acquireStaticLock(context);

    context.startService(new Intent(context, AppService.class));
  }
}
```

While there is very little code in this class, it is merely deceptively simple.

First, we acquire a `WakeLock` from our `AppService`'s parent class, `WakefulIntentService` via `acquireStaticLock()`, shown below:

```java
public static void acquireStaticLock(Context context) {
  getLock(context).acquire();
}

synchronized private static PowerManager.WakeLock getLock(Context context) {
  if (lockStatic==null) {
    PowerManager
mgr=(PowerManager)context.getSystemService(Context.POWER_SERVICE);

    lockStatic=mgr.newWakeLock(PowerManager.PARTIAL_WAKE_LOCK,
                     LOCK_NAME_STATIC);
    lockStatic.setReferenceCounted(true);
  }

  return(lockStatic);
}
```

The `getLock()` implementation lazy-creates our `WakeLock` by getting the `PowerManager`, creating a new partial `WakeLock`, and setting it to be reference counted (meaning if it is acquired several times, it takes a corresponding number of `release()` calls to truly release the lock). If we have already retrieved the `WakeLock` in a previous invocation, we reuse the same lock.

Back in `OnAlarmReceiver`, up until this point, the CPU was running because `AlarmManager` held a partial `WakeLock`. Now, the CPU is running because both `AlarmManager` *and* `WakefulIntentService` hold a partial `WakeLock`.

Then, `OnAlarmReceiver` starts the `AppService` instance (remember: `acquireStaticLock()` was a *static* method) and exits. Notably,

`OnAlarmReceiver` does not release the `WakeLock` it acquired. This is important, as we need to ensure that the service can get its work done while the CPU is running. Had we released the `WakeLock` before returning, it is possible that the device would fall back asleep before our service had a chance to acquire a fresh `WakeLock`. This is one of the keys of using `WakeLock` successfully – as needed, use overlapping `WakeLock` instances to ensure constant coverage as you pass from component to component.

Now, our service will start up and be able to do something, while the CPU is running due to our acquired `WakeLock`.

Staying Awake At Work

So, `AppService` will now get control, under an active `WakeLock`. At minimum, our service will be called via `onStart()`, and possibly also `onCreate()` if the service had been previously stopped. Our mission is to do our work and release the `WakeLock`.

Since services should not do long-running tasks in `onStart()`, we could fork a `Thread`, have it do the work in the background, then have it release the `WakeLock`. Note that we cannot release the `WakeLock` in `onStart()` in this case – just because we have a background thread does not mean the device will keep the CPU running.

There are issues with forking a `Thread` for every incoming request, though:

- If the work needed to be done sometimes takes longer than the alarm period, we could wind up with many background threads, which is inefficient. It also means our `WakeLock` management gets much trickier, since we will not have released the `WakeLock` before the alarm tries to `acquire()` it again.
- If we also are invoked in `onStart()` via some foreground activity, we might wind up with many more bits of work to be done, again causing confusion with our `WakeLock` and perhaps slowing things down due to too many background threads.

Android has a class that helps with parts of this, `IntentService`. It arranges for a work queue of inbound `Intents` – rather than overriding `onStart()`, you override `onHandleIntent()`, which is called from a background thread. Android handles all the details of shutting down your service when there is no more outstanding work, managing the background thread, and so on.

However, `IntentService` does not do anything to hold a `WakeLock`.

Hence, this sample project implements `WakefulIntentService` as a subclass of `IntentService`. `WakefulIntentService` handles most of the `WakeLock` logic, so `AppService` (inheriting from `WakefulIntentService`) can just focus on the work it needs to do.

`WakefulIntentService` handles the `WakeLock` logic in four components:

1. It offers the public static method `acquireStaticLock()`, which needs to be called by whoever is calling `startService()` on our `WakefulIntentService` subclass.

2. In `onCreate()`, it creates (but does not acquire) another `WakeLock`. The static `WakeLock` will be used to keep the device awake while the `BroadcastReceiver` (or whoever else is calling `startService()`) starts up the service. The local `WakeLock` will be used to keep the device awake so long as there is work to be done.

3. In `onStart()`, it acquires the local `WakeLock`, lets the superclass do its work to enqueue the supplied Intent for later processing, then releases the static `WakeLock`. At this point, the device still must remain awake, because even though the `AlarmManager WakeLock` (used during the call to `onReceive()` in our `BroadcastReceiver`) is released, and our static `WakeLock` is released, our local `WakeLock` is still held.

4. In `onHandleIntent()`, it releases the local `WakeLock`. Since this `WakeLock` is reference-counted, the lock will only fully release once every `Intent` enqueued by `onStart()` has been handled by `onHandleIntent()`.

Here is the full implementation of `WakefulIntentService`:

```java
package com.commonsware.android.syssvc.alarm;

import android.app.AlarmManager;
import android.app.PendingIntent;
import android.app.IntentService;
import android.content.Context;
import android.content.Intent;
import android.os.IBinder;
import android.os.PowerManager;
import android.util.Log;

public class WakefulIntentService extends IntentService {
  public static final String
LOCK_NAME_STATIC="com.commonsware.android.syssvc.AppService.Static";
  public static final String
LOCK_NAME_LOCAL="com.commonsware.android.syssvc.AppService.Local";
  private static PowerManager.WakeLock lockStatic=null;
  private PowerManager.WakeLock lockLocal=null;

  public static void acquireStaticLock(Context context) {
```

Using System Services

```java
    getLock(context).acquire();
  }

  synchronized private static PowerManager.WakeLock getLock(Context context) {
    if (lockStatic==null) {
      PowerManager
mgr=(PowerManager)context.getSystemService(Context.POWER_SERVICE);

      lockStatic=mgr.newWakeLock(PowerManager.PARTIAL_WAKE_LOCK,
                        LOCK_NAME_STATIC);
      lockStatic.setReferenceCounted(true);
    }

    return(lockStatic);
  }

  public WakefulIntentService(String name) {
    super(name);
  }

  public void onCreate() {
    super.onCreate();

    PowerManager mgr=(PowerManager)getSystemService(Context.POWER_SERVICE);

    lockLocal=mgr.newWakeLock(PowerManager.PARTIAL_WAKE_LOCK,
                        LOCK_NAME_LOCAL);
    lockLocal.setReferenceCounted(true);
  }

  @Override
  public void onStart(Intent intent, final int startId) {
    lockLocal.acquire();

    super.onStart(intent, startId);

    getLock(this).release();
  }

  @Override
  protected void onHandleIntent(Intent intent) {
    lockLocal.release();
  }
}
```

With all that behind us, `AppService` need only implement `onHandleIntent()`, do its work, and then chain upward to the `WakefulIntentService`'s implementation of `onHandleIntent()`:

```java
package com.commonsware.android.syssvc.alarm;

import android.content.Intent;
```

Using System Services

```java
import android.os.Environment;
import android.util.Log;
import java.io.BufferedWriter;
import java.io.File;
import java.io.FileWriter;
import java.io.IOException;
import java.util.Date;

public class AppService extends WakefulIntentService {
  public AppService() {
    super("AppService");
  }

  @Override
  protected void onHandleIntent(Intent intent) {
    File log=new File(Environment.getExternalStorageDirectory(),
                      "AlarmLog.txt");

    try {
      BufferedWriter out=new BufferedWriter(new
FileWriter(log.getAbsolutePath(), true));

      out.write(new Date().toString());
      out.write("\n");
      out.close();
    }
    catch (IOException e) {
      Log.e("AppService", "Exception appending to log file", e);
    }

    super.onHandleIntent(intent);
  }
}
```

The "fake work" being done by this `AppService` is simply logging the fact that work needed to be done to a log file on the SD card.

Note that if you attempt to build and run this project that you will need an SD card in the device (or card image attached to your emulator).

Setting Expectations

If you have an Android device, you probably have spent some time in the Settings application, tweaking your device to work how you want – ringtones, WiFi settings, USB debugging, etc. Many of those settings are also available via `Settings` class (in the `android.provider` package), and particularly the `Settings.System` and `Settings.Secure` public inner classes.

Basic Settings

`Settings.System` allows you to get and, with the `WRITE_SETTINGS` permission, alter these settings. As one might expect, there are a series of typed getter and setter methods on `Settings.System`, each taking a key as a parameter. The keys are class constants, such as:

- `INSTALL_NON_MARKET_APPS` to control whether you can install applications on a device from outside of the Android Market
- `LOCK_PATTERN_ENABLED` to control whether the user needs to enter a lock pattern to enable use of the device
- `LOCK_PATTERN_VISIBLE` to control whether the lock pattern is drawn on-screen as it is swiped by the user, or if the swipes are "invisible"

The `SystemServices/Settings` project has a `SettingsSetter` sample application that displays a checklist:

```xml
<?xml version="1.0" encoding="utf-8"?>
<ListView xmlns:android="http://schemas.android.com/apk/res/android"
  android:id="@android:id/list"
  android:layout_width="fill_parent"
  android:layout_height="fill_parent"
/>
```

Using System Services

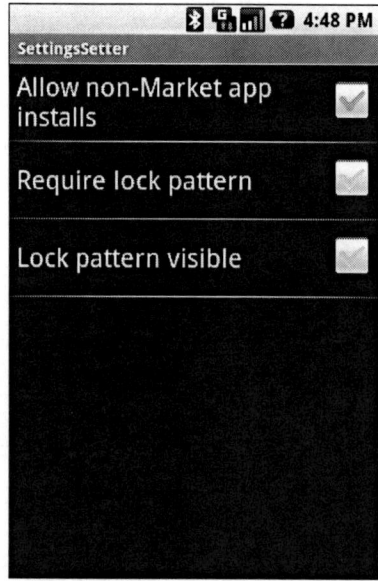

Figure 42. The SettingsSetter application

The checklist itself is filled with a few `BooleanSetting` objects, which map a display name with a `Settings.System` key:

```
static class BooleanSetting {
  String key;
  String displayName;

  BooleanSetting(String key, String displayName) {
    this.key=key;
    this.displayName=displayName;
  }

  @Override
  public String toString() {
    return(displayName);
  }

  boolean isChecked(ContentResolver cr) {
    try {
      int value=Settings.System.getInt(cr, key);

      return(value!=0);
    }
    catch (Settings.SettingNotFoundException e) {
      Log.e("SettingsSetter", e.getMessage());
    }

    return(false);
```

Using System Services

```
  }
  void setChecked(ContentResolver cr, boolean value) {
    Settings.System.putInt(cr, key, (value ? 1 : 0));
  }
}
```

Three such settings are put in the list, and as the checkboxes are checked and unchecked, the values are passed along to the settings themselves:

```
@Override
public void onCreate(Bundle savedInstanceState) {
  super.onCreate(savedInstanceState);
  setContentView(R.layout.main);

  getListView().setChoiceMode(ListView.CHOICE_MODE_MULTIPLE);
  setListAdapter(new ArrayAdapter(this,
                    android.R.layout.simple_list_item_multiple_choice,
                    settings));

  ContentResolver cr=getContentResolver();

  for (int i=0;i<settings.size();i++) {
    BooleanSetting s=settings.get(i);

    getListView().setItemChecked(i, s.isChecked(cr));
  }
}

@Override
protected void onListItemClick(ListView l, View v,
                    int position, long id) {
  super.onListItemClick(l, v, position, id);

  BooleanSetting s=settings.get(position);

  s.setChecked(getContentResolver(),
          l.isItemChecked(position));
}
```

The `SettingsSetter` activity also has an option menu containing four items:

```
<?xml version="1.0" encoding="utf-8"?>
<menu xmlns:android="http://schemas.android.com/apk/res/android">
  <item android:id="@+id/app"
    android:title="Application"
    android:icon="@android:drawable/ic_menu_manage" />
  <item android:id="@+id/security"
    android:title="Security"
    android:icon="@android:drawable/ic_menu_close_clear_cancel" />
```

Using System Services

```xml
  <item android:id="@+id/wireless"
    android:title="Wireless"
    android:icon="@android:drawable/ic_menu_set_as" />
  <item android:id="@+id/all"
    android:title="All Settings"
    android:icon="@android:drawable/ic_menu_preferences" />
</menu>
```

These items correspond to four activity `Intent` values identified by the `Settings` class:

```java
menuActivities.put(R.id.app,
                Settings.ACTION_APPLICATION_SETTINGS);
menuActivities.put(R.id.security,
                Settings.ACTION_SECURITY_SETTINGS);
menuActivities.put(R.id.wireless,
                Settings.ACTION_WIRELESS_SETTINGS);
menuActivities.put(R.id.all,
                Settings.ACTION_SETTINGS);
```

When an option menu is chosen, the corresponding activity is launched:

```java
@Override
public boolean onOptionsItemSelected(MenuItem item) {
  String activity=menuActivities.get(item.getItemId());

  if (activity!=null) {
    startActivity(new Intent(activity));

    return(true);
  }

  return(super.onOptionsItemSelected(item));
}
```

This way, you have your choice of either directly manipulating the settings or merely making it easier for users to get to the Android-supplied activity for manipulating those settings.

Secure Settings

You will notice that if you use the above code and try changing the value of "Allow non-Market app installs", the change does not "stick" – once you exit and reopen the application, the setting returns to its original state.

Using System Services

Moreover, if you use the Settings application and examine the setting, it is clear that SettingsSetter is not actually changing that particular setting.

Once upon a time – Android 1.1 and earlier – it did.

Now, though, that setting is one that Android deems "secure". The constant has been moved from Settings.System to Settings.Secure, though the old constant is still there, flagged as deprecated.

These so-called "secure" settings are one that Android does not allow applications to change. No permission resolves this problem. The only option is to display the official Settings activity and let the user change the setting.

Can You Hear Me Now? OK, How About Now?

The fancier the device, the more complicated controlling sound volume becomes.

On a simple MP3 player, there is usually only one volume control. That is because there is only one source of sound: the music itself, played through speakers or headphones.

In Android, though, there are several sources of sounds:

- Ringing, to signify an incoming call
- Voice calls
- Alarms, such as those raised by the Alarm Clock application
- System sounds (error beeps, USB connection signal, etc.)
- Music, as might come from the MP3 player

Android allows the user to configure each of these volume levels separately. Usually, the user does this via the volume rocker buttons on the device, in the context of whatever sound is being played (e.g., when on a call, the

Using System Services

volume buttons change the voice call volume). Also, there is a screen in the Android Settings application that allows you to configure various volume levels.

The `AudioService` in Android allows you, the developer, to also control these volume levels, for all five "streams" (i.e., sources of sound). In the `SystemServices/Volume` project, we create a `Volumizer` application that displays and modifies all five volume levels, reusing the `Meter` widget we created in an earlier chapter.

Reusing Meter

Given that `Meter` was originally developed in a separate project, we had to do a few things to make it usable here.

First, we had to copy over the layout (`res/layout/meter.xml`), source (`src/com/commonsware/android/widget/Meter.java`), and two `Drawable` resources (`res/drawable/incr.png` and `res/drawable/decr.png`). We then moved it all into the same package as everything else (`com.commonsware.android.syssvc.volume`).

This, of course, defeats much of the reusability. Once better widget reuse models become apparent, expect updates to this book to cover them.

Attaching Meters to Volume Streams

Given that we have our `Meter` widget to work with, setting up `Meter` widgets to work with volume streams is fairly straightforward.

First, we need to create a layout with a `Meter` per stream:

```
<?xml version="1.0" encoding="utf-8"?>
<TableLayout xmlns:android="http://schemas.android.com/apk/res/android"
  xmlns:app="http://schemas.android.com/apk/res/com.commonsware.android.syssvc.v
olume"
  android:stretchColumns="1"
  android:layout_width="fill_parent"
```

Using System Services

```xml
    android:layout_height="fill_parent"
  >
  <TableRow
    android:paddingTop="10px"
    android:paddingBottom="20px">
    <TextView android:text="Alarm:" />
    <com.commonsware.android.syssvc.volume.Meter
      android:id="@+id/alarm"
      android:layout_width="fill_parent"
      android:layout_height="wrap_content"
      app:incr="1"
      app:decr="1"
    />
  </TableRow>
  <TableRow
    android:paddingBottom="20px">
    <TextView android:text="Music:" />
    <com.commonsware.android.syssvc.volume.Meter
      android:id="@+id/music"
      android:layout_width="fill_parent"
      android:layout_height="wrap_content"
      app:incr="1"
      app:decr="1"
    />
  </TableRow>
  <TableRow
    android:paddingBottom="20px">
    <TextView android:text="Ring:" />
    <com.commonsware.android.syssvc.volume.Meter
      android:id="@+id/ring"
      android:layout_width="fill_parent"
      android:layout_height="wrap_content"
      app:incr="1"
      app:decr="1"
    />
  </TableRow>
  <TableRow
    android:paddingBottom="20px">
    <TextView android:text="System:" />
    <com.commonsware.android.syssvc.volume.Meter
      android:id="@+id/system"
      android:layout_width="fill_parent"
      android:layout_height="wrap_content"
      app:incr="1"
      app:decr="1"
    />
  </TableRow>
  <TableRow>
    <TextView android:text="Voice:" />
    <com.commonsware.android.syssvc.volume.Meter
      android:id="@+id/voice"
      android:layout_width="fill_parent"
      android:layout_height="wrap_content"
      app:incr="1"
```

```
      app:decr="1"
    />
  </TableRow>
</TableLayout>
```

Then, we need to wire up each of those meters in the onCreate() for Volumizer:

```
Meter alarm=null;
Meter music=null;
Meter ring=null;
Meter system=null;
Meter voice=null;
AudioManager mgr=null;

@Override
public void onCreate(Bundle savedInstanceState) {
  super.onCreate(savedInstanceState);
  setContentView(R.layout.main);

  mgr=(AudioManager)getSystemService(Context.AUDIO_SERVICE);

  alarm=(Meter)findViewById(R.id.alarm);
  music=(Meter)findViewById(R.id.music);
  ring=(Meter)findViewById(R.id.ring);
  system=(Meter)findViewById(R.id.system);
  voice=(Meter)findViewById(R.id.voice);

  alarm.setTag(AudioManager.STREAM_ALARM);
  music.setTag(AudioManager.STREAM_MUSIC);
  ring.setTag(AudioManager.STREAM_RING);
  system.setTag(AudioManager.STREAM_SYSTEM);
  voice.setTag(AudioManager.STREAM_VOICE_CALL);

  initMeter(alarm);
  initMeter(music);
  initMeter(ring);
  initMeter(system);
  initMeter(voice);
}
```

We use the tag for each Meter to hold the identifier for the stream associated with that specific Meter. That way, each Meter knows its stream.

In initMeter(), we set the appropriate size for the Meter bar via setMax(), set the initial value via setProgress(), and wire our increment and decrement events to the appropriate methods on VolumeManager:

Using System Services

```java
    final int stream=((Integer)meter.getTag()).intValue();

  meter.setMax(mgr.getStreamMaxVolume(stream));
  meter.setProgress(mgr.getStreamVolume(stream));
  meter.setOnIncrListener(new View.OnClickListener() {
    public void onClick(View v) {
      mgr.adjustStreamVolume(stream,
                             AudioManager.ADJUST_RAISE, 0);
    }
  });
  meter.setOnDecrListener(new View.OnClickListener() {
    public void onClick(View v) {
      mgr.adjustStreamVolume(stream,
                             AudioManager.ADJUST_LOWER, 0);
    }
  });
  }
}
```

The net result is that when the user clicks the buttons on a meter, it adjusts the stream to match:

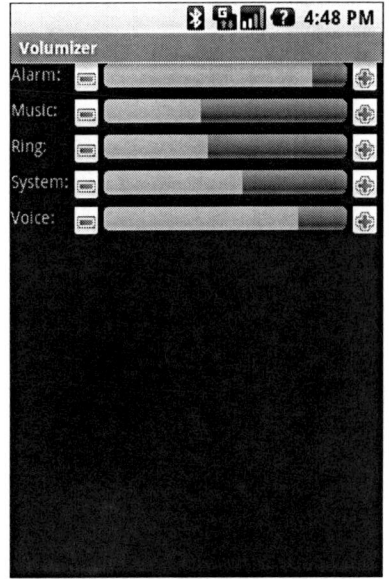

Figure 43. The Volumizer application

CHAPTER 13

Your Own (Advanced) Services

In *The Busy Coder's Guide to Android Development*, we covered how to create and consume services. Now, we can get into some more interesting facets of service implementations, notably remote services, so your service can serve activities outside of your application.

When IPC Attacks!

Services will tend to offer inter-process communication (IPC) as a means of interacting with activities or other Android components. Each service declares what methods it is making available over IPC; those methods are then available for other components to call, with Android handling all the messy details involved with making method calls across component or process boundaries.

The guts of this, from the standpoint of the developer, is expressed in AIDL: the Android Interface Description Language. If you have used IPC mechanisms like COM, CORBA, or the like, you will recognize the notion of IDL. AIDL describes the public IPC interface, and Android supplies tools to build the client and server side of that interface.

With that in mind, let's take a look at AIDL and IPC.

Write the AIDL

IDLs are frequently written in a "language-neutral" syntax. AIDL, on the other hand, looks a lot like a Java interface. For example, here is some AIDL:

```
package com.commonsware.android.advservice;

// Declare the interface.
interface IScript {
  void executeScript(String script);
}
```

As with a Java interface, you declare a package at the top. As with a Java interface, the methods are wrapped in an interface declaration (`interface IScript { ... }`). And, as with a Java interface, you list the methods you are making available.

The differences, though, are critical.

First, not every Java type can be used as a parameter. Your choices are:

- Primitive values (`int`, `float`, `double`, `boolean`, etc.)
- `String` and `CharSequence`
- `List` and `Map` (from `java.util`)
- Any other AIDL-defined interfaces
- Any Java classes that implement the `Parcelable` interface, which is Android's flavor of serialization

In the case of the latter two categories, you need to include `import` statements referencing the names of the classes or interfaces that you are using (e.g., `import com.commonsware.android.ISomething`). This is true even if these classes are in your own package – you have to import them anyway.

Next, parameters can be classified as `in`, `out`, or `inout`. Values that are `out` or `inout` can be changed by the service and those changes will be propagated back to the client. Primitives (e.g., int) can only be in; we included in for the AIDL for enable() just for illustration purposes.

Also, you cannot throw any exceptions. You will need to catch all exceptions in your code, deal with them, and return failure indications some other way (e.g., error code return values).

Name your AIDL files with the .aidl extension and place them in the proper directory based on the package name.

When you build your project, either via an IDE or via Ant, the aidl utility from the Android SDK will translate your AIDL into a server stub and a client proxy.

Implement the Interface

Given the AIDL-created server stub, now you need to implement the service, either directly in the stub, or by routing the stub implementation to other methods you have already written.

The mechanics of this are fairly straightforward:

- Create a private instance of the AIDL-generated .Stub class (e.g., IScript.Stub)
- Implement methods matching up with each of the methods you placed in the AIDL
- Return this private instance from your onBind() method in the Service subclass

Note that AIDL IPC calls are synchronous, and so the caller is blocked until the IPC method returns. Hence, your services need to be quick about their work.

We will see examples of service stubs later in this chapter.

A Consumer Economy

Of course, we need to have a client for AIDL-defined services, lest these services feel lonely.

Bound for Success

To use an AIDL-defined service, you first need to create an instance of your own `ServiceConnection` class. `ServiceConnection`, as the name suggests, represents your connection to the service for the purposes of making IPC calls.

Your `ServiceConnection` subclass needs to implement two methods:

1. `onServiceConnected()`, which is called once your activity is bound to the service
2. `onServiceDisconnected()`, which is called if your connection ends normally, such as you unbinding your activity from the service

Each of those methods receives a `ComponentName`, which simply identifies the service you connected to. More importantly, `onServiceConnected()` receives an `IBinder` instance, which is your gateway to the IPC interface. You will want to convert the `IBinder` into an instance of your AIDL interface class, so you can use IPC as if you were calling regular methods on a regular Java class (`IScript.Stub.asInterface(binder)`).

To actually hook your activity to the service, call `bindService()` on the activity:

```
bindService(new Intent(IScript.class.getName()),
            svcConn, Context.BIND_AUTO_CREATE);
```

The `bindService()` method takes three parameters:

1. An `Intent` representing the service you wish to invoke
2. Your `ServiceConnection` instance

3. A set of flags – most times, you will want to pass in BIND_AUTO_CREATE, which will start up the service if it is not already running

After your `bindService()` call, your `onServiceConnected()` callback in the `ServiceConnection` will eventually be invoked, at which time your connection is ready for use.

Request for Service

Once your service interface object is ready (`IScript.Stub.asInterface(binder)`), you can start calling methods on it as you need to. In fact, if you disabled some widgets awaiting the connection, now is a fine time to re-enable them.

However, you will want to trap two exceptions. One is `DeadObjectException` – if this is raised, your service connection terminated unexpectedly. In this case, you should unwind your use of the service, perhaps by calling `onServiceDisconnected()` manually, as shown above. The other is `RemoteException`, which is a more general-purpose exception indicating a cross-process communications problem. Again, you should probably cease your use of the service.

Prometheus Unbound

When you are done with the IPC interface, call `unbindService()`, passing in the `ServiceConnection`. Eventually, your connection's `onServiceDisconnected()` callback will be invoked, at which point you should null out your interface object, disable relevant widgets, or otherwise flag yourself as no longer being able to use the service.

You can always reconnect to the service, via `bindService()`, if you need to use it again.

Service From Afar

Everything from the preceding two sections could be used by local services. In fact, that prose originally appeared in *The Busy Coder's Guide to Android Development* specifically in the context of local services. However, AIDL adds a fair bit of overhead, which is not necessary with local services. After all, AIDL is designed to marshal its parameters and transport them across process boundaries, which is why there are so many quirky rules about what you can and cannot pass as parameters to your AIDL-defined APIs.

So, given our AIDL description, let us examine some implementations, specifically for remote services.

Our sample applications – shown in the AdvServices/RemoteService and AdvServices/RemoteClient sample projects – convert our Beanshell demo from *The Busy Coder's Guide to Android Development* into a remote service. If you actually wanted to use scripting in an Android application, with scripts loaded off of the Internet, isolating their execution into a service might not be a bad idea. In the service, those scripts are sandboxed, only able to access files and APIs available to that service. The scripts cannot access your own application's databases, for example. If the script-executing service is kept tightly controlled, it minimizes the mischief a rogue script could possibly do.

Service Names

To bind to a service's AIDL-defined API, you need to craft an Intent that can identify the service in question. In the case of a local service, that Intent can use the local approach of directly referencing the service class.

Obviously, that is not possible in a remote service case, where the service class is not in the same process, and may not even be known by name to the client.

When you define a service to be used by remote, you need to add an intent-filter element to your service declaration in the manifest, indicating how

Your Own (Advanced) Services

you want that service to be referred to by clients. The manifest for `RemoteService` is shown below:

```xml
<?xml version="1.0" encoding="utf-8"?>
<manifest xmlns:android="http://schemas.android.com/apk/res/android"
    package="com.commonsware.android.advservice"
    android:versionCode="1"
    android:versionName="1.0">
  <application android:label="@string/app_name">
    <service android:name=".BshService">
      <intent-filter>
        <action android:name="com.commonsware.android.advservice.IScript" />
      </intent-filter>
    </service>
  </application>
</manifest>
```

Here, we say that the service can be identified by the name `com.commonsware.android.advservice.IScript`. So long as the client uses this name to identify the service, it can bind to that service's API.

In this case, the name is not an implementation, but the AIDL API, as you will see below. In effect, this means that so long as some service exists on the device that implements this API, the client will be able to bind to something.

The Service

Beyond the manifest, the service implementation is not too unusual. There is the AIDL interface, `IScript`:

```
package com.commonsware.android.advservice;

// Declare the interface.
interface IScript {
  void executeScript(String script);
}
```

And there is the actual service class itself, `BshService`:

```
package com.commonsware.android.advservice;

import android.app.Service;
```

```java
import android.content.Intent;
import android.os.IBinder;
import android.util.Log;
import bsh.Interpreter;

public class BshService extends Service {
  private final IScript.Stub binder=new IScript.Stub() {
    public void executeScript(String script) {
      executeScriptImpl(script);
    }
  };
  private Interpreter i=new Interpreter();

  @Override
  public void onCreate() {
    super.onCreate();

    try {
      i.set("context", this);
    }
    catch (bsh.EvalError e) {
      Log.e("BshService", "Error executing script", e);
    }
  }

  @Override
  public IBinder onBind(Intent intent) {
    return(binder);
  }

  @Override
  public void onDestroy() {
    super.onDestroy();
  }

  private void executeScriptImpl(String script) {
    try {
      i.eval(script);
    }
    catch (bsh.EvalError e) {
      Log.e("BshService", "Error executing script", e);
    }
  }
}
```

If you have seen the service and Beanshell samples in then this implementation will seem familiar. The biggest thing to note is that the service returns no result and handles any errors locally. Hence, the client will not get any response back from the script – the script will just run. In a real implementation, this would be silly, and we will work to rectify this later in this chapter.

Your Own (Advanced) Services

Also note that, in this implementation, the script is executed directly by the service on the calling thread. One might think this is not a problem, since the service is in its own process and, therefore, cannot possibly be using the client's UI thread. However, AIDL IPC calls are synchronous, so the client will still block waiting for the script to be executed. This too will be corrected later in this chapter.

The Client

The client – `BshServiceDemo` out of `AdvServices/RemoteClient` – is a fairly straight-forward mashup of the service and Beanshell clients, with two twists:

```
package com.commonsware.android.advservice.client;

import android.app.Activity;
import android.app.AlertDialog;
import android.content.ComponentName;
import android.content.Context;
import android.content.Intent;
import android.content.ServiceConnection;
import android.os.Bundle;
import android.os.IBinder;
import android.view.View;
import android.widget.Button;
import android.widget.EditText;
import com.commonsware.android.advservice.IScript;

public class BshServiceDemo extends Activity {
  private IScript service=null;
  private ServiceConnection svcConn=new ServiceConnection() {
    public void onServiceConnected(ComponentName className,
                                   IBinder binder) {
      service=IScript.Stub.asInterface(binder);
    }

    public void onServiceDisconnected(ComponentName className) {
      service=null;
    }
  };

  @Override
  public void onCreate(Bundle icicle) {
    super.onCreate(icicle);
    setContentView(R.layout.main);

    Button btn=(Button)findViewById(R.id.eval);
    final EditText script=(EditText)findViewById(R.id.script);
```

```
  btn.setOnClickListener(new View.OnClickListener() {
    public void onClick(View view) {
      String src=script.getText().toString();

      try {
        service.executeScript(src);
      }
      catch (android.os.RemoteException e) {
        AlertDialog.Builder builder=
                new AlertDialog.Builder(BshServiceDemo.this);

        builder
          .setTitle("Exception!")
          .setMessage(e.toString())
          .setPositiveButton("OK", null)
          .show();
      }
    }
  });

  bindService(new Intent(IScript.class.getName()),
          svcConn, Context.BIND_AUTO_CREATE);
}

@Override
public void onDestroy() {
  super.onDestroy();

  unbindService(svcConn);
}
}
```

One twist is that the client needs its own copy of IScript.aidl. After all, it is a totally separate application, and therefore does not share source code with the service. In a production environment, we might craft and distribute a JAR file that contains the IScript classes, so both client and service can work off the same definition (see the upcoming chapter on reusable components). For now, we will just have a copy of the AIDL.

Then, the bindService() call uses a slightly different Intent, one that references the name of the AIDL interface's class implementation. That happens to be the name the service is registered under, and that is the glue that allows the client to find the matching service.

If you compile both applications and upload them to the device, then start up the client, you can enter in Beanshell code and have it be executed by the service. Note, though, that you cannot perform UI operations (e.g., raise a `Toast`) from the service. If you choose some script that is long-running, you will see that the Go! button is blocked until the script is complete:

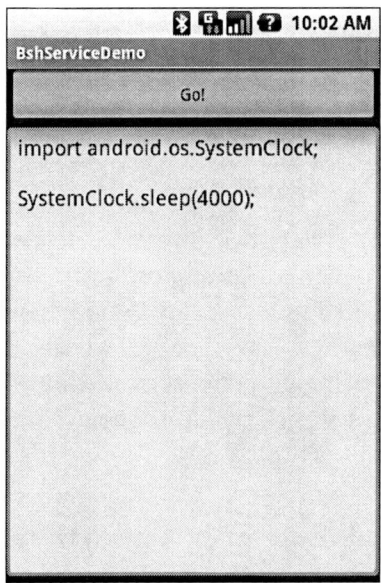

Figure 44. The BshServiceDemo application, running a long script

Servicing the Service

The preceding section outlined two flaws in the implementation of the Beanshell remote service:

1. The client received no results from the script execution
2. The client blocked waiting for the script to complete

If we were not worried about the blocking-call issue, we could simply have the `executeScript()` exported API return some sort of result (e.g., `toString()` on the result of the Beanshell `eval()` call). However, that would not solve the fact that calls to service APIs are synchronous even for remote services.

Another approach would be to pass some sort of callback object with `executeScript()`, such that the server could run the script asynchronously and invoke the callback on success or failure. This, though, implies that there is some way to have the activity export an API to the service.

Fortunately, this is eminently doable, as you will see in this section, and the accompanying samples (`AdvServices/RemoteServiceEx` and `AdvServices/RemoteClientEx`).

Callbacks via AIDL

AIDL does not have any concept of direction. It just knows interfaces and stub implementations. In the preceding example, we used AIDL to have the service flesh out the stub implementation and have the client access the service via the AIDL-defined interface. However, there is nothing magic about services implementing and clients accessing – it is equally possible to reverse matters and have the client implement something the service uses via an interface.

So, for example, we could create an `IScriptResult.aidl` file:

```
package com.commonsware.android.advservice;

// Declare the interface.
interface IScriptResult {
  void success(String result);
  void failure(String error);
}
```

Then, we can augment `IScript` itself, to pass an `IScriptResult` with `executeScript()`:

```
package com.commonsware.android.advservice;

import com.commonsware.android.advservice.IScriptResult;

// Declare the interface.
interface IScript {
  void executeScript(String script, IScriptResult cb);
}
```

Notice that we need to specifically import `IScriptResult`, just like we might import some "regular" Java interface. And, as before, we need to make sure

Your Own (Advanced) Services

the client and the server are working off of the same AIDL definitions, so these two AIDL files need to be replicated across each project.

But other than that one little twist, this is all that is required, at the AIDL level, to have the client pass a callback object to the service: define the AIDL for the callback and add it as a parameter to some service API call.

Of course, there is a little more work to do on the client and server side to make use of this callback object.

Revising the Client

On the client, we need to implement an IScriptResult. On success(), we can do something like raise a Toast; on failure(), we can perhaps show an AlertDialog.

The catch is that we cannot be certain we are being called on the UI thread in our callback object.

So, the safest way to do that is to make the callback object use something like runOnUiThread() to ensure the results are displayed on the UI thread:

```
private final IScriptResult.Stub callback=new IScriptResult.Stub() {
  public void success(final String result) {
    runOnUiThread(new Runnable() {
      public void run() {
        successImpl(result);
      }
    });
  }

  public void failure(final String error) {
    runOnUiThread(new Runnable() {
      public void run() {
        failureImpl(error);
      }
    });
  }
};

private void successImpl(String result) {
  Toast
```

```
      .makeText(BshServiceDemo.this, result, Toast.LENGTH_LONG)
      .show();
}

private void failureImpl(String error) {
  AlertDialog.Builder builder=
          new AlertDialog.Builder(BshServiceDemo.this);

  builder
    .setTitle("Exception!")
    .setMessage(error)
    .setPositiveButton("OK", null)
    .show();
}
```

And, of course, we need to update our call to `executeScript()` to pass the callback object to the remote service:

```
@Override
public void onCreate(Bundle icicle) {
  super.onCreate(icicle);
  setContentView(R.layout.main);

  Button btn=(Button)findViewById(R.id.eval);
  final EditText script=(EditText)findViewById(R.id.script);

  btn.setOnClickListener(new View.OnClickListener() {
    public void onClick(View view) {
      String src=script.getText().toString();

      try {
        service.executeScript(src, callback);
      }
      catch (android.os.RemoteException e) {
        failureImpl(e.toString());
      }
    }
  });

  bindService(new Intent(IScript.class.getName()),
          svcConn, Context.BIND_AUTO_CREATE);
}
```

Revising the Service

The service also needs changing, to both execute the scripts asynchronously and use the supplied callback object for the end results of the script's execution.

Your Own (Advanced) Services

As was demonstrated in the chapter on `Camera`, `BshService` from `AdvServices/RemoteServiceEx` uses the `LinkedBlockingQueue` pattern to manage a background thread. An `ExecuteScriptJob` wraps up the script and callback; when the job is eventually processed, it uses the callback to supply the results of the `eval()` (on success) or the message of the `Exception` (on failure):

```java
package com.commonsware.android.advservice;

import android.app.Service;
import android.content.Intent;
import android.os.IBinder;
import android.util.Log;
import java.util.concurrent.LinkedBlockingQueue;
import bsh.Interpreter;

public class BshService extends Service {
  private final IScript.Stub binder=new IScript.Stub() {
    public void executeScript(String script, IScriptResult cb) {
      executeScriptImpl(script, cb);
    }
  };
  private Interpreter i=new Interpreter();
  private LinkedBlockingQueue<Job> q=new LinkedBlockingQueue<Job>();

  @Override
  public void onCreate() {
    super.onCreate();

    new Thread(qProcessor).start();

    try {
      i.set("context", this);
    }
    catch (bsh.EvalError e) {
      Log.e("BshService", "Error executing script", e);
    }
  }

  @Override
  public IBinder onBind(Intent intent) {
    return(binder);
  }

  @Override
  public void onDestroy() {
    super.onDestroy();

    q.add(new KillJob());
  }

  private void executeScriptImpl(String script,
```

```
                                          IScriptResult cb) {
    q.add(new ExecuteScriptJob(script, cb));
}

Runnable qProcessor=new Runnable() {
    public void run() {
        while (true) {
            try {
                Job j=q.take();

                if (j.stopThread()) {
                    break;
                }
                else {
                    j.process();
                }
            }
            catch (InterruptedException e) {
                break;
            }
        }
    }
};

class Job {
    boolean stopThread() {
        return(false);
    }

    void process() {
        // no-op
    }
}

class KillJob extends Job {
    @Override
    boolean stopThread() {
        return(true);
    }
}

class ExecuteScriptJob extends Job {
    IScriptResult cb;
    String script;

    ExecuteScriptJob(String script, IScriptResult cb) {
        this.script=script;
        this.cb=cb;
    }

    void process() {
        try {
            cb.success(i.eval(script).toString());
        }
```

```
      catch (Throwable e) {
        Log.e("BshService", "Error executing script", e);

        try {
          cb.failure(e.getMessage());
        }
        catch (Throwable t) {
          Log.e("BshService",
                "Error returning exception to client",
                t);
        }
      }
    }
   }
  }
}
```

Notice that the service's own API just needs the `IScriptResult` parameter, which can be passed around and used like any other Java object. The fact that it happens to cause calls to be made synchronously back to the remote client is invisible to the service.

The net result is that the client can call the service and get its results without tying up the client's UI thread.

CHAPTER 14

Finding Available Actions via Introspection

Sometimes, you know just what you want to do, such as display one of your other activities.

Sometimes, you have a pretty good idea of what you want to do, such as view the content represented by a Uri, or have the user pick a piece of content of some MIME type.

Sometimes, you're lost. All you have is a content Uri, and you don't really know what you can do with it.

For example, suppose you were creating a common tagging subsystem for Android, where users could tag pieces of content – contacts, Web URLs, geographic locations, etc. Your subsystem would hold onto the Uri of the content plus the associated tags, so other subsystems could, say, ask for all pieces of content referencing some tag.

That's all well and good. However, you probably need some sort of maintenance activity, where users could view all their tags and the pieces of content so tagged. This might even serve as a quasi-bookmark service for items on their phone. The problem is, the user is going to expect to be able to do useful things with the content they find in your subsystem, such as dial a contact or show a map for a location.

Finding Available Actions via Introspection

The problem is, you have absolutely no idea what is all possible with any given content Uri. You probably can view any of them, but can you edit them? Can you dial them? Since new applications with new types of content could be added by any user at any time, you can't even assume you know all possible combinations just by looking at the stock applications shipped on all Android devices.

Fortunately, the Android developers thought of this.

Android offers various means by which you can present to your users a set of likely activities to spawn for a given content Uri...even if you have no idea what that content Uri really represents. This chapter explores some of these Uri action introspection tools.

Pick 'Em

Sometimes, you know your content Uri represents a collection of some type, such as content://contacts/people representing the list of contacts in the stock Android contacts list. In this case, you can let the user pick a contact that your activity can then use (e.g., tag it, dial it).

To do this, you need to create an intent for the ACTION_PICK on the target Uri, then start a sub activity (via startActivityForResult()) to allow the user to pick a piece of content of the specified type. If your onActivityResult() callback for this request gets a RESULT_OK result code, your data string can be parsed into a Uri representing the chosen piece of content.

For example, take a look at Introspection/Pick in the sample applications. This activity gives you a field for a collection Uri (with content://contacts/people pre-filled in for your convenience), plus a really big "Gimme!" button:

```
<?xml version="1.0" encoding="utf-8"?>
<LinearLayout xmlns:android="http://schemas.android.com/apk/res/android"
    android:orientation="vertical"
    android:layout_width="fill_parent"
    android:layout_height="fill_parent"
    >
```

Finding Available Actions via Introspection

```xml
<EditText android:id="@+id/type"
    android:layout_width="fill_parent"
    android:layout_height="wrap_content"
    android:cursorVisible="true"
    android:editable="true"
    android:singleLine="true"
    android:text="content://contacts/people"
/>
<Button
    android:id="@+id/pick"
    android:layout_width="fill_parent"
    android:layout_height="fill_parent"
    android:text="Gimme!"
    android:layout_weight="1"
/>
</LinearLayout>
```

Upon being clicked, the button creates the ACTION_PICK on the user-supplied collection Uri and starts the sub-activity. When that sub-activity completes with RESULT_OK, the ACTION_VIEW is invoked on the resulting content Uri.

```java
public class PickDemo extends Activity {
    static final int PICK_REQUEST=1337;
    private EditText type;

    @Override
    public void onCreate(Bundle icicle) {
        super.onCreate(icicle);
        setContentView(R.layout.main);
        type=(EditText)findViewById(R.id.type);

        Button btn=(Button)findViewById(R.id.pick);

        btn.setOnClickListener(new View.OnClickListener() {
            public void onClick(View view) {
                Intent i=new Intent(Intent.ACTION_PICK,
                        Uri.parse(type.getText().toString()));

                startActivityForResult(i, PICK_REQUEST);
            }
        });
    }

    @Override
    protected void onActivityResult(int requestCode, int resultCode,
                                    Intent data) {
        if (requestCode==PICK_REQUEST) {
            if (resultCode==RESULT_OK) {
                startActivity(new Intent(Intent.ACTION_VIEW,
                        data.getData()));
```

Finding Available Actions via Introspection

```
        }
      }
    }
}
```

The result: the user chooses a collection, picks a piece of content, and views it.

Figure 45. The PickDemo sample application, as initially launched

Finding Available Actions via Introspection

Figure 46. The same application, after clicking the "Gimme!" button, showing the list of available people

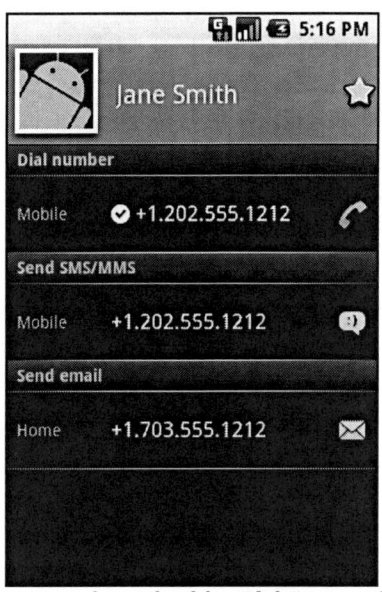

Figure 47. A view of a contact, launched by PickDemo after choosing one of the people from the pick list

Would You Like to See the Menu?

Another way to give the user ways to take actions on a piece of content, without you knowing what actions are possible, is to inject a set of menu choices into the options menu via `addIntentOptions()`. This method, available on `Menu`, takes an `Intent` and other parameters and fills in a set of menu choices on the `Menu` instance, each representing one possible action. Choosing one of those menu choices spawns the associated activity.

The canonical example of using `addIntentOptions()` illustrates another flavor of having a piece of content and not knowing the actions that can be taken. Android applications are perfectly capable of adding new actions to existing content types, so even though you wrote your application and know what you expect to be done with your content, there may be other options you are unaware of that are available to users.

For example, imagine the tagging subsystem mentioned in the introduction to this chapter. It would be very annoying to users if, every time they wanted to tag a piece of content, they had to go to a separate tagging tool, then turn around and pick the content they just had been working on (if that is even technically possible) before associating tags with it. Instead, they would probably prefer a menu choice in the content's own "home" activity where they can indicate they want to tag it, which leads them to the set-a-tag activity and tells that activity what content should get tagged.

To accomplish this, the tagging subsystem should set up an intent filter, supporting any piece of content, with their own action (e.g., `ACTION_TAG`) and a category of `CATEGORY_ALTERNATIVE`. The category `CATEGORY_ALTERNATIVE` is the convention for one application adding actions to another application's content.

If you want to write activities that are aware of possible add-ons like tagging, you should use `addIntentOptions()` to add those add-ons' actions to your options menu, such as the following:

```
Intent intent = new Intent(null, myContentUri);
```

Finding Available Actions via Introspection

```
intent.addCategory(Intent.ALTERNATIVE_CATEGORY);
menu.addIntentOptions(Menu.ALTERNATIVE, 0,
                new ComponentName(this,
                                  MyActivity.class),
                null, intent, 0, null);
```

Here, myContentUri is the content Uri of whatever is being viewed by the user in this activity, MyActivity is the name of the activity class, and menu is the menu being modified.

In this case, the Intent we are using to pick actions from requires that appropriate intent receivers support the CATEGORY_ALTERNATIVE. Then, we add the options to the menu with addIntentOptions() and the following parameters:

- The sort position for this set of menu choices, typically set to 0 (appear in the order added to the menu) or ALTERNATIVE (appear after other menu choices)

- A unique number for this set of menu choices, or 0 if you do not need a number

- A ComponentName instance representing the activity that is populating its menu – this is used to filter out the activity's own actions, so the activity can handle its own actions as it sees fit

- An array of Intent instances that are the "specific" matches – any actions matching those intents are shown first in the menu before any other possible actions

- The Intent for which you want the available actions

- A set of flags. The only one of likely relevance is represented as MATCH_DEFAULT_ONLY, which means matching actions must also implement the DEFAULT_CATEGORY category. If you do not need this, use a value of 0 for the flags.

- An array of Menu.Item, which will hold the menu items matching the array of Intent instances supplied as the "specifics", or null if you do not need those items (or are not using "specifics")

Asking Around

The addIntentOptions() method in turn uses queryIntentActivityOptions() for the "heavy lifting" of finding possible actions. The queryIntentActivityOptions() method is implemented on PackageManager, which is available to your activity via getPackageManager().

The queryIntentActivityOptions() method takes some of the same parameters as does addIntentOptions(), notably the caller ComponentName, the "specifics" array of Intent instances, the overall Intent representing the actions you are seeking, and the set of flags. It returns a List of Intent instances matching the stated criteria, with the "specifics" ones first.

If you would like to offer alternative actions to users, but by means other than addIntentOptions(), you could call queryIntentActivityOptions(), get the Intent instances, then use them to populate some other user interface (e.g., a toolbar).

PART IV – Advanced Development

CHAPTER 15

Testing

Presumably, you will want to test your code, beyond just playing around with it yourself by hand.

To that end, Android includes the JUnit test framework in the SDK, along with special test classes that will help you build test cases that exercise Android components, like activities and services. Even better, Android 1.5 has "gone the extra mile" and can pre-generate your test harness for you, to make it easier for you to add in your own tests.

This chapter assumes you have some familiarity with JUnit, though you certainly do not need to be an expert. You can learn more about JUnit at the JUnit site[27], from various books, and from the JUnit Yahoo forum[28].

You Get What They Give You

When you create a project in Android 1.5 using android create project, Android automatically creates a new tests/ directory inside the project directory. If you look in there, you will see a complete set of Android project artifacts: manifest, source directories, resources, etc. This is actually a test project, designed to partner with the main project to create a complete testing solution.

---

27 http://www.junit.org/
28 http://tech.groups.yahoo.com/group/junit

Testing

In fact, that test project is all ready to go, other than not having any tests of significance. If you build and install your main project (onto an emulator or device), then build and install the test project, you will be able to run unit tests.

Android ships with a very rudimentary JUnit runner, called `InstrumentationTestRunner`. Since this class resides in the Android environment (emulator or device), you need to invoke the runner to run your tests on the emulator or device itself. To do this, you can run the following command from a console:

```
adb shell am instrument -w
com.commonsware.android.database.tests/android.test.InstrumentationTestRunner
```

In this case, we are instructing Android to run all the available test cases for the `com.commonsware.android.database` package, as this chapter uses some tests implemented on the `Database/Contacts` sample project.

If you were to run this on your own project, substituting in your package name, with just the auto-generated test files, you should see results akin to:

```
com.commonsware.android.database.ContactsDemoTest:.
Test results for InstrumentationTestRunner=.
Time: 0.61

OK (1 test)
```

The first line will differ, based upon your package and the name of your project's initial activity, but the rest should be the same, showing that a single test was run, successfully.

Of course, this is only the beginning.

Erecting More Scaffolding

Here is the source code for the test case that Android automatically generates for you:

Testing

```java
package com.commonsware.android.database;

import android.test.ActivityInstrumentationTestCase;
/**
 * This is a simple framework for a test of an Application. See
 * {@link android.test.ApplicationTestCase ApplicationTestCase} for more information on
 * how to write and extend Application tests.
 * <p/>
 * To run this test, you can type:
 * adb shell am instrument -w \
 * -e class com.commonsware.android.database.ContactsDemoTest \
 * com.commonsware.android.database.tests/android.test.InstrumentationTestRunner
 */
public class ContactsDemoTest extends
ActivityInstrumentationTestCase<ContactsDemo> {

  public ContactsDemoTest() {
    super("com.commonsware.android.database", ContactsDemo.class);
  }

}
```

As you can see, there are no actual test methods. Instead, we have an `ActivityInstrumentationTestCase` implementation named `ContactsDemoTest`. The class name was generated by adding Test to the end of the main activity (`ContactsDemo`) of the project.

In the next section, we will examine `ActivityInstrumentationTestCase` more closely and see how you can use it to, as the name suggests, test your activities.

However, you are welcome to create ordinary JUnit test cases in Android – after all, this is just JUnit, merely augmented by Android. So, you can create classes like this:

```java
package com.commonsware.android.database;

import junit.framework.TestCase;

public class SillyTest extends TestCase {
  protected void setUp() throws Exception {
    super.setUp();

    // do initialization here, run on every test method
  }
```

Testing

```
protected void tearDown() throws Exception {
  // do termination here, run on every test method

  super.tearDown();
}
public void testNonsense() {
  assertTrue(1==1);
}
}
```

There is nothing Android-specific in this test case. It is simply standard JUnit, albeit a bit silly.

You can also create test suites, to bundle up sets of tests for execution. Here, though, if you want, you can take advantage of a bit of Android magic: `TestSuiteBuilder`. `TestSuiteBuilder` uses reflection to find test cases that need to be run, as shown below:

```
package com.commonsware.android.database;

import android.test.suitebuilder.TestSuiteBuilder;
import junit.framework.Test;
import junit.framework.TestSuite;

public class FullSuite extends TestSuite {
  public static Test suite() {
    return(new TestSuiteBuilder(FullSuite.class)
              .includeAllPackagesUnderHere()
              .build());
  }
}
```

Here, we are telling Android to find all test cases located in `FullSuite`'s package (`com.commonsware.android.database`) and all sub-packages, and to build a `TestSuite` out of those contents.

A test suite may or may not be necessary for you. The command shown above to execute tests will execute any test cases it can find for the package specified on the command line. If you want to limit the scope of a test run, though, you can use the `-e` switch to specify a test case or suite to run:

```
adb shell am instrument -e class
com.commonsware.android.database.ContactsDemoTest -w
com.commonsware.android.database.tests/android.test.InstrumentationTestRunner
```

Here, we indicate we only want to run `ContactsDemoTest`, not all test cases found in the package.

Testing Real Stuff

While ordinary JUnit tests are certainly helpful, they are still fairly limited, since much of your application logic may be tied up in activities, services, and the like.

To that end, Android has a series of `TestCase` classes you can extend designed specifically to assist in testing these sorts of components.

ActivityInstrumentationTestCase

The test case created by Android's SDK tools, `ContactsDemoTest` in our example, is an `ActivityInstrumentationTestCase`. This class will run your activity for you, giving you access to the `Activity` object itself. You can then:

- Access your widgets
- Invoke public and package-private methods (more on this below)
- Simulate key events

Of course, the automatically-generated `ActivityInstrumentationTestCase` does none of that, since it does not know much about your activity. Below you will find an augmented version of `ContactsDemoTest` that does a little bit more:

```
package com.commonsware.android.database;

import android.test.ActivityInstrumentationTestCase;
import android.widget.ListView;
import android.widget.Spinner;

public class ContactsDemoTest
```

```
extends ActivityInstrumentationTestCase<ContactsDemo> {
  private ListView list=null;
  private Spinner spinner=null;

  public ContactsDemoTest() {
    super("com.commonsware.android.database",
          ContactsDemo.class);
  }

  @Override
  protected void setUp() throws Exception {
    super.setUp();

    ContactsDemo activity=getActivity();

    list=(ListView)activity.findViewById(android.R.id.list);
    spinner=(Spinner)activity.findViewById(R.id.spinner);
  }

  public void testSpinnerCount() {
    assertTrue(spinner.getAdapter().getCount()==3);
  }

  public void testListDefaultCount() {
    assertTrue(list.getAdapter().getCount()>0);
  }
}
```

Here are the steps to making use of `ActivityInstrumentationTestCase`:

1. Extend the class to create your own implementation. Since `ActivityInstrumentationTestCase` is a generic, you need to supply the name of the activity being tested (e.g., `ActivityInstrumentationTestCase<ContactsDemo>`).

2. In the constructor, when you chain to the superclass, supply the name of the package of the activity plus the activity class itself. You can optionally supply a third parameter, a boolean indicating if the activity should be launched in touch mode or not.

3. In `setUp()`, use `getActivity()` to get your hands on your `Activity` object, already typecast to the proper type (e.g., `ContactsDemo`) courtesy of our generic. You can also at this time access any widgets, since the activity is up and running by this point.

4. If needed, clean up stuff in `tearDown()`, no different than with any other JUnit test case.

Testing

5. Implement test methods to exercise your activity. In this case, we simply confirm that the Spinner has three items in its drop-down list and there is at least one contact loaded into the ListView by default. You could, however, use sendKeys() and the like to simulate user input.

If you are looking at your emulator or device while this test is running, you will actually see the activity launched on-screen. ActivityInstrumentationTestCase creates a true running copy of the activity. This means you get access to everything you need; on the other hand, it does mean that the test case runs slowly, since the activity needs to be created and destroyed for each test method in the test case. If your activity does a lot on startup and/or shutdown, this may make running your tests a bit sluggish.

Note that your ActivityInstrumentationTestCase resides in the same package as the Activity it is testing – ContactsDemoTest and ContactsDemo are both in com.commonsware.android.database, for example. This allows ContactsDemoTest to access both public and package-private methods and data members. ContactsDemoTest still cannot access private methods, though. This allows ActivityInstrumentationTestCase to behave in a white-box (or at least gray-box) fashion, inspecting the insides of the tested activities in addition to testing the public API.

Now, despite the fact that Android's own tools create an ActivityInstrumentationTestCase subclass for you, that class is officially deprecated. They advise using ActivityInstrumentationTestCase2 instead, which offers the same basic functionality, with a few extras, such as being able to specify the Intent that is used to launch the activity being tested. This is good for testing search providers, for example.

AndroidTestCase

For tests that only need access to your application resources, you can skip some of the overhead of ActivityInstrumentationTestCase and use AndroidTestCase. In AndroidTestCase, you are given a Context and not much

Testing

more, so anything you can reach from a `Context` is testable, but individual activities or services are not.

While this may seem somewhat useless, bear in mind that a lot of the static testing of your activities will come in the form of testing the layout: are the widgets identified properly, are they positioned properly, does the focus work, etc. As it turns out, none of that actually needs an `Activity` object – so long as you can get the inflated `View` hierarchy, you can perform those sorts of tests.

For example, here is an `AndroidTestCase` implementation, `ContactsDemoBaseTest`:

```java
package com.commonsware.android.database;

import android.test.AndroidTestCase;
import android.view.LayoutInflater;
import android.view.View;
import android.view.ViewGroup;
import android.widget.ListView;
import android.widget.Spinner;

public class ContactsDemoBaseTest extends AndroidTestCase {
  private ListView list=null;
  private Spinner spinner=null;
  private ViewGroup root=null;

  @Override
  protected void setUp() throws Exception {
    super.setUp();

    LayoutInflater inflater=LayoutInflater.from(getContext());

    root=(ViewGroup)inflater.inflate(R.layout.main, null);
    root.measure(480, 320);
    root.layout(0, 0, 480, 320);

    list=(ListView)root.findViewById(android.R.id.list);
    spinner=(Spinner)root.findViewById(R.id.spinner);
  }

  public void testExists() {
    assertNotNull(list);
    assertNotNull(spinner);
  }

  public void testRelativePosition() {
    assertTrue(list.getTop()>=spinner.getBottom());
```

```
    assertTrue(list.getLeft()==spinner.getLeft());
    assertTrue(list.getRight()==spinner.getRight());
  }
}
```

Most of the complicated work is performed in setUp():

1. Inflate our layout using a LayoutInflater and the Context supplied by getContext()
2. Measure and lay out the widgets in the inflated View hierarchy – in this case, we lay them out on a 480x320 screen
3. Access the individual widgets to be tested

At that point, we can test static information on the widgets, but we cannot cause them to change very easily (e.g., we cannot simulate keypresses). In the case of ContactsDemoBaseTest, we simply confirm the widgets exist and are laid out as expected. We could use FocusFinder to test whether focus changes from one widget to the next should work as expected. We could ensure our resources exist under their desired names, test to see if our fonts exist in our assets, or anything else we can accomplish with just a Context.

Since we are not creating and destroying activities with each test case, these tests should run substantially faster.

Other Alternatives

Android also offers various other test case base classes designed to assist in testing Android components, such as:

- ServiceTestCase, used for testing services, as you might expect given the name
- ActivityUnitTestCase, a TestCase that creates the Activity (like ActivityInstrumentationTestCase), but does not fully connect it to the environment, so you can supply a mock Context, a mock Application, and other mock objects to test out various scenarios
- ApplicationTestCase, for testing custom Application subclasses

Monkeying Around

Independent from the JUnit system is the Monkey.

The Monkey is a test program that simulates random user input. It is designed for "bash testing", confirming that no matter what the user does, the application will not crash. The application may have odd results – random input entered into a Twitter client may, indeed, post that random input to Twitter. The Monkey does not test to make sure that results of random input make sense; it only tests to make sure random input does not blow up the program.

You can run the Monkey by setting up your initial starting point (e.g., the main activity in your application) on your device or emulator, then running a command like this:

```
adb shell monkey -p com.commonsware.android.database -v --throttle 100 600
```

Working from right to left, we are asking for 600 simulated events, throttled to run every 100 milliseconds. We want to see a list of the invoked events (-v) and we want to throw out any event that might cause the Monkey to leave our application, as determined by the application's package (-p com.commonsware.android.database).

The Monkey will simulate keypresses (both QWERTY and specialized hardware keys, like the volume controls), D-pad/trackball moves, and sliding the keyboard open or closed. Note that the latter may cause your emulator some confusion, as the emulator itself does not itself actually rotate, so you may end up with your screen appearing in landscape while the emulator is still, itself, portrait. Just rotate the emulator a couple of times (e.g., <Ctrl>-<F12>) to clear up the problem.

For playing with a Monkey, the above command works fine. However, if you want to regularly test your application this way, you may need some measure of repeatability. After all, the particular set of input events that trigger your crash may not come up all that often, and without that repeatable scenario, it will be difficult to repair the bug, let alone test that the repair worked.

To deal with this, the Monkey offers the -s switch, where you provide a seed for the random number generator. By default, the Monkey creates its own seed, giving totally random results. If you supply the seed, while the sequence of events is random, it is random for that seed – repeatedly using the same seed will give you the same events. If you can arrange to detect a crash and know what seed was used to create that crash, you may well be able to reproduce the crash.

There are many more Monkey options, to control the mix of event types, to generate profiling reports as tests are run, and so on. The Monkey documentation[29] in the SDK's Developer's Guide covers all of that and more.

---

29 http://developer.android.com/guide/developing/tools/monkey.html

Keyword Index

Class

AccelerateDecelerateInterpolator...................95

AccelerateInterpolator......................................95

Activity......16, 50, 124, 168-170, 179, 229, 230, 232, 233

ActivityInstrumentationTestCase...227, 229-231, 233

ActivityInstrumentationTestCase2.................231

ActivityUnitTestCase..233

Adapter..30-32, 35, 36, 146

AdapterView.OnItemSelectedListener............46

AlarmManager........66, 168, 179, 180, 182, 183, 185

AlertDialog...209

AlphaAnimation...............................87, 92-94, 97

AnalogClock...50

AndroidTestCase.......................................231, 232

Animation..87, 88, 94-96

AnimationListener.......................................94, 95

AnimationSet...87, 96, 97

AnimationUtils..94

Application...233

ApplicationTestCase...233

AppService....................................182-185, 187, 188

AppWidgetHost..66

AppWidgetHostView..66

AppWidgetManager..............................56, 61, 65

AppWidgetProvider........................55, 59, 64, 65

AsyncTask..119

AttributeSet...16

AudioService..193

BaseColumns..150

BatteryMonitor..174, 176

BitmapDrawable..120

BooleanSetting...189

BroadcastReceiver. 50-52, 55, 65, 66, 169-171, 173, 181, 182, 185

BroadcastReciever..55

BshService...203, 211

BshServiceDemo..205

Button.............21, 23, 24, 40, 50, 51, 58, 75, 76, 82

CallLog...150, 152, 153, 160

Keyword Index

CallLog.Calls..150

CallPlusAdapter...158, 160

Camera................................113-115, 117-119, 211

Camera.Parameters....................................115, 117

Camera.PictureCallback....................................119

Camera.ShutterCallback....................................118

CharSequence..198

CheckBox..21, 25, 27

Chronometer..50

ComponentName.....................56, 200, 221, 222

ConstantsInstaller...141

Contacts..142, 143, 150

Contacts.ContactMethodsColumns..............149

Contacts.PeopleColumns........................148, 149

Contacts.Phones..148

Contacts.PhonesColumns...............................148

ContactsDemo...................143, 147, 227, 230, 231

ContactsDemoBaseTest........................232, 233

ContactsDemoTest..........................227, 229, 231

ContentProvider......................................151, 168

ContentValues..157

Context..............16, 94, 124, 130, 170, 179, 231-233

Cursor............................31, 151-153, 156, 157, 160

CursorAdapter...158

CursorJoiner..152

CursorWrapper..151, 152

CycleInterpolator......................................94, 96

DatabaseInstaller.....................................140-142

DeadObjectException.....................................201

DecelerateInterpolator......................................95

Drawable..............................23-26, 42, 71, 72, 193

Drawable/GradientDemo................................72

EditText..51

Exception...211

ExecuteScriptJob...211

FocusFinder...233

FrameLayout..50

FullSuite..228

GeoWebOne...2

HeaderFooterDemo..38

I_JoinHandler...156, 157

IBinder..200

ImageButton................13, 15, 19, 50, 51, 55, 58, 95

ImageView..50, 173

InputStream..141

InstrumentationTestRunner..........................226

Intent. .x, 55, 60, 61, 66, 167-171, 173-175, 179, 180, 182, 185, 191, 200, 206, 220-222, 231

IntentService.......................................56, 66, 185

Interpolator..95, 96

IScript...203, 206, 208

IScriptResult...208, 209, 213

JoinCache..157

JoinCursor...................................152, 153, 156-158

JoinDemo...151, 157, 158, 160

LayoutInflater..58, 233

LinearInterpolator..95

LinearLayout..15, 38, 50, 89, 90

LinkedBlockingQueue...................................211

LinkedHashMap...157

List..35, 198, 222

238

Keyword Index

ListActivity..................32, 36, 43, 143, 160

ListView. 29-32, 36, 38, 42, 43, 46, 57, 72, 74, 143, 144, 160, 231

Locater..4

LocationListener..4, 8

LocationManager..4

Map..198

Media/Audio..101

MediaPlayer.....................100, 101, 104, 105

Menu..94, 220

Menu.Item..221

Meter......................13-16, 18, 19, 21, 193, 195

MeterDemo..21

MyActivity...221

NinePatchDemo..82

NoteActivity..165

NoteEditor...165

OnAlarmReceiver..................................182-184

OnBootCompleted......................................169

OnBootReceiver...................................169, 181

OnClickListener...51

OnWiFiChangeReceiver..............................171

PackageManager...222

Parcelable..198

PendingIntent............................51, 58, 179, 182

PhotoCallback...120

PictureDemo..118, 120

PowerManager....................................180, 183

PreferenceActivity..................................58, 60

PreviewDemo......................................112, 113

ProgressBar....................13, 14, 50, 173, 176

RelativeLayout...50

RemoteException..201

RemoteService..203

RemoteViews................50, 51, 55-59, 61

RotateAnimation....................................87, 94

SavePhotoTask....................................119, 120

ScaleAnimation..87

ScrollView...128

Section...35

SectionAdapter..35

SectionedAdapter............................32, 35, 36

SectionedDemo....................................32, 36

SeekBar..13, 82

SelectorAdapter..46

SelectorDemo..43, 46

SelectorWrapper..46

Sensor...125

SensorEvent..125

SensorEventListener............................125, 127

SensorManager...........................124, 125, 130

Service.............50-52, 56, 66, 168, 179, 199

ServiceConnection...............................200, 201

ServiceTestCase..233

Settings...188, 191

Settings.Secure...................................188, 192

Settings.System...........................188, 189, 192

SettingsSetter...........................188, 190, 192

Shaker..129-131

Shaker.Callback..131

ShakerDemo..129, 131

Keyword Index

SharedPreferences..58

SimpleCursorAdapter...................31, 32, 146, 149

SlidingPanel......................................90, 92, 94-96

SlidingPanelDemo..91

Spinner..143, 144, 146, 231

SQLiteDatabase..141

SQLiteOpenHelper..........................137, 140, 141

String..198

SurfaceHolder..113, 114

SurfaceHolder.Callback...........................114, 115

SurfaceView..113-115

TestCase..229, 233

TestSuite..228

TestSuiteBuilder...228

TextSwitcher...88

TextView..27, 40, 43, 46, 50, 55, 58, 126, 128, 129, 173, 176

Thread..184

Toast..207, 209

TranslateAnimation............87-90, 92, 93, 95, 97

TranslationAnimation......................................94

TwitterWidget................................54-56, 64-66

TWPrefs..58, 59

TypedArray..17

UpdateService..56, 57

Uri..99, 100, 215-217, 221

VideoDemo...107

VideoView..105, 106

View..30-32, 35, 36, 38, 40, 42, 43, 46, 49, 50, 57, 58, 66, 88, 94, 232, 233

View.OnClickListener......................................18

ViewAnimator..88

ViewFlipper...88

ViewWrapper..158

VolumeManager...195

Volumizer..193, 195

WakefulIntentService.......................183, 185, 187

WakeLock...................................180, 183-185

WebSettings...1

WebView..................................1, 2, 4, 7, 9, 10

WebViewClient..1

WidgetProvider..61

Command......................................

adb push..107

draw9patch...78, 79, 83

mksdcard...107

sqlite3...138, 139, 141

Constant..

ACTION_PICK......................................216, 217

ACTION_TAG..220

ACTION_VIEW..217

ALTERNATIVE...221

BIND_AUTO_CREATE....................................201

CATEGORY_ALTERNATIVE..................220, 221

DEFAULT_CATEGORY....................................221

MATCH_DEFAULT_ONLY..............................221

RESULT_OK...216, 217

Method...

acquire()...184

Keyword Index

acquireStaticLock()..........................183, 185
addFooterView()..38
addHeaderView()..38
addIntentOptions()................................220-222
addJavascriptInterface()......................2, 4, 6
addSection()..35
areAllItemsSelectable()..................................30
bindService()...................................200-202, 206
buildFooter()..40
buildHeader()...40
buildUpdate()..56, 57
create()..104
delete()..135
doInBackground()..120
enable()..199
eval()..207, 211
execSQL()..141, 142
executeScript()..............................207, 208, 210
failure()...209
findViewById()..57
getActivity()...230
getColumnCount()..157
getColumnIndex()..157
getContext()...233
getCount()..35
getHolder()..114
getInt()..17, 157
getItem()...35
getItemViewType()...................................35, 36
getJoin()..157, 158

getLock()..183
getPackageManager()...................................222
getSystemService().........................124, 179, 182
getView()..32, 35
getViewTypeCount()................................35, 36
handleInstallError()......................................141
initMeter()..195
insert()..135
isEnabled()..30
isNull()..157
loadAnimation()..94
loadUrl()...7, 9
obtainStyledAttributes()..........................16, 17
onAccuracyChanged()..................................125
onActivityResult()..216
onAnimationEnd()..94
onBind()..199
onClick()...19
onCreate()....................104, 114, 141, 184, 185, 195
onDeleted()...65, 66
onDestroy()..60, 125
onDisabled()...65
onEnabled()...65
onFinishInflate()..16, 17
onHandleIntent()..............................56, 185, 187
onItemSelected()..46
onKeyDown()......................................60, 61, 117
onLocationChanged()......................................8
onNothingSelected()..46
onPause()..174

241

Keyword Index

onPictureTaken()......................................119
onReceive()...........................65, 66, 170, 182, 185
onResume()...174
onSensorChanged()..................................125
onServiceConnected()..........................200, 201
onServiceDisconnected()......................200, 201
onStart()..184, 185
onUpdate()....................................55, 64, 65
onUpgrade()...141
open()..113
pause()..101, 105
play()..105
prepare()..101, 104
prepareAsync().....................................101
query()..135
queryIntentActivityOptions()....................222
recycle()..17
registerListener()...................................125
registerReceiver()..................168, 169, 171, 173
release()....................................105, 115, 183
requery()..157, 158
runOnUiThread()...................................209
sendKeys()...231
setAnimationListener()..............................94
setDataSource()....................................101
setDuration()..92
setInterpolator()....................................96
setMax()..195
setOnClickPendingIntent()........................58
setOnItemSelectedListener().......................43

setPictureFormat()..................................117
setPreviewDisplay()................................114
setProgress()..195
setRepeating().......................................182
setResult()...61
setTextViewText()..................................58
setType()..114
setup()..104, 105
setUp()..230, 233
setVisibility()....................................89, 94
shakingStarted()....................................131
shakingStopped()..................................131
start()..101
startActivityForResult().......................59, 216
startAnimation()................................88, 92
startPreview()......................................115
startService()...........................56, 170, 185
steerLeft()...128
steerRight()..128
stop()...101, 105
stopPreview()......................................115
success()..209
surfaceChanged()..................................115
surfaceCreated()...................................114
surfaceDestroyed()................................115
takePicture().......................................118
tearDown()..230
toggle()..90
toString()...207
unbindService()....................................201

242

Keyword Index

unregisterListener()..125

update()..135

updateAppWidget()..............................56, 61, 65